THE SYNAGOGUE

לזכר נשמת עדיאל ע״ה
In memory of Adiel

JPS Popular Judaica Library

General Editor: Raphael Posner

THE SYNAGOGUE

Edited by Uri Kaploun

JEWISH PUBLICATION SOCIETY OF AMERICA

Philadelphia, Pa.

Copyright © Israel Program for Scientific Translations Ltd., 1973

First published in Israel by KETER BOOKS, an imprint of
ISRAEL PROGRAM FOR SCIENTIFIC TRANSLATIONS LTD.
P.O. Box 7145, Jerusalem

Published by
THE JEWISH PUBLICATION SOCIETY OF AMERICA
222 N. 15th St., Philadelphia, Pa. 19102

Library of Congress Catalogue Card 72 13537
ISBN 0 8276   0012 7
All rights reserved

Manufactured by Keter Press, Jerusalem, Israel 1973

Printed in Israel

CONTENTS

INTRODUCTION

1. A LITTLE SANCTUARY 1
ORIGINS: Prayer and Sacrifice – The Temple. FIRST CENTURY. ANCIENT SYNA-
GOGUES OUTSIDE EREZ ISRAEL. THE SYNAGOGUE AT THE TEMPLE. THE *Bet
Midrash.* BODY AND SOUL. ORDER OF SERVICE. AFTER THE TEMPLE. EDUCATION.
IN *Aggadah.*

2. THE PULSE OF THE COMMUNITY 10
PHILANTHROPY: *Pletten.* ADMINISTRATION: Communal Legislation. DEMOC-
RACY: Leadership. THE *Ḥazzan:* Qualifications. THE RABBI: Qualifications –
Functions – Governmental Interference – Pastoral Activities – The *Dayyan* –
The State of Israel. THE PREACHER: Jacob Kranz – *Shabbat* – Preaching in the
Vernacular – Subjects of Sermons – The State of Israel. THE READER OF THE
LAW. THE *Shammash.*

3. IN THE MULTITUDE OF PEOPLE IS THE KING'S GLORY 27
THE *Ḥasidim:* The *Rebbe.* THE SOCIAL STRUCTURE OF THE SYNAGOGUE: Syna-
gogues by Profession – Names. THE REFORM MOVEMENT: The Organ. THE
ORIENTAL SYNAGOGUE: Spontaneity – The Yemenite Synagogue – The Bukharan
Synagogue – The Persian Synagogue – Cochin. THE STATE OF ISRAEL: The
Army. THE SOVIET BLOC: The Yevsektsiya – Underground – The Revival –
Present Conditions   The Rest of the Bloc.

4. THOSE WHO MOURN THE DESTRUCTION
WILL SURELY REJOICE AT THE REBUILDING 43
ANCIENT TIMES. THE MIDDLE AGES. MOHAMMEDAN LANDS. THE HOLOCAUST:
Statistics and Documentation. THE OLD CITY OF JERUSALEM: The Ramban
Synagogue – The Yoḥanan ben Zakkai Synagogue – The Ḥurva Synagogue –
The Ḥabad Synagogue.

5. OLD WINE IN NEW VESSELS 53
THE EARLY YEARS. ASSIMILATION. THE JEWISH CENTER: Program – Affiliated
Clubs – Special Sabbaths – Education – Microphones – Expanding Synagogues.
SYNAGOGUE ORGANIZATIONS: England – The United States – The State of
Israel. STATISTICS.

6. TO EXALT THE HOUSE OF OUR LORD   60
WATER. HEIGHT. ORIENTATION. THE VESTIBULE. WINDOWS. SEPARATE SEAT-
ING: *Weibershul* – The *Zoggeren* – Abolition of the *Meḥiẓah*.

7. BEHOLD THEY HAD DONE IT
AS THE LORD HAD COMMANDED   66
USE OF THE SYNAGOGUE: Behavior – Gambling – Cleanliness. HOLINESS OF
CEREMONIAL OBJECTS. OWNERSHIP AND DISPOSAL. WEDDINGS IN THE SYNA-
GOGUE. FESTIVALS IN THE SYNAGOGUE.

8. HEAVEN AND THE HEAVEN OF HEAVENS
CANNOT CONTAIN THEE   71
EARLY SYNAGOGUES: The Transitional Type – Fifth-Century Synagogues – Out-
side Ereẓ Israel. FROM THE MIDDLE AGES TO THE EIGHTEENTH CENTURY: Forma-
tion of the Interior – The Double-Naved Hall – The Single-Cell Hall – Renaissance
and Baroque Influences – The Four-Pillared Hall – Synagogues as Fortresses –
Wooden Synagogues – Spain – Arab Countries – Italy. THE NINETEENTH
CENTURY. THE EARLY TWENTIETH CENTURY. THE CONTEMPORARY PERIOD.
IN EUROPE AFTER WORLD WAR II.

9. THIS IS MY GOD AND I WILL GLORIFY HIM   99
SYMBOLISM. THE TORAH SCROLL: The Garments – The Breastplate – The *Yad* –
The Wrapper. THE ARK: The *Parokhet* – The *Ner Tamid* – Candelabra. THE
Bimah – Position. THE *Ammud*.

GLOSSARY   .   110

SOURCES   113

BIBLIOGRAPHY   117

INTRODUCTION

No institution has been so vital or central in Jewish life as the synagogue. During its long history it has assumed different roles and functions as the needs of the community it served have changed, but it has always been the dynamo from which the Jewish people has drawn its inner power. The Jew came to the synagogue to pray to God, to seek inspiration and to achieve and maintain his own identity. Judaism would be unthinkable without the synagogue—whether stately edifice or humble prayer-room— and no substitute for it has yet been found.

In the twentieth century the condition of the Jewish people has undergone the most rapid and extreme changes of its history since the destruction of the Second Temple in 70 C.E. The beginning of the present century saw the unprecedented migration of huge masses of Jews from Eastern Europe to the United States. That journey must be measured in more than mere miles; overnight, as it were, a good part of the Jewish people came face to face with the modern age. As the century completed its first third, the horror of Nazism reared its monstrous head and the Jewish people suffered the greatest single catastrophe it had ever known. Eastern and Central Europe ceased to exist from the Jewish point of view; the great reservoir of Jewish culture, scholarship and piety that had been patiently and painstakingly created over centuries was wiped out in a few short years. Out of the ashes of the holocaust a phoenix arose—the State of Israel, which has added a new dimension to Jewish life.

Jewish history has always presented a mystery and for no period so much as for this century. What is the secret of Jewish survival? Why is this people so different from the other peoples which have disappeared from the stage of human history? The thinking Jew who is pondering the mystery of Jewish existence must take the synagogue into consideration, for it has been a constant factor in all periods and in all places where Jews have been. Perhaps such a consideration may enlighten with regard to the future, too.

The synagogue can only be fitted into the scheme of things if something is known about its history and functions. This book is intended to help achieve that aim. Scores of books have been written about all the various aspects of the synagogue and it is certainly not the purpose of this little book to provide a comprehensive treatment of such a wide subject. Rather, we have tried to present a brief, clear and straightforward picture in the hope that it will whet the reader's appetite to go further. To that purpose, a bibliography is appended as is a list of the main sources referred to in the text. If that hope is realized, this book will have served its purpose well.

1. A LITTLE SANCTUARY

One evening during the Australian gold rush of 1853, a dozen homesick Jews banded together in a humble shanty on the edge of the Ballarat diggings, and there chanted the prayers of Rosh ha-Shanah. Perhaps it was the self-same song that found a path through the sad hearts of the Babylonian exiles when, sick for home, they sought a substitute on alien soil for the despoiled Temple of Jerusalem. Seeking consolation in their distress, they would no doubt meet to read the Scriptures, probably on Sabbaths, for it was thus that they could feel that the Divine Presence accompanied them in their wanderings.

Origins

The Jews who had remained in Judea after the Exile of Jehoiachin in 597 B.C.E. taunted these expatriates for their distance from the Temple, and Ezekiel answered, "Thus saith the Lord God: 'Although I have removed them far off among the nations, and although I have scattered them among the countries, yet have I been to them as a little sanctuary in the countries where they are come.'" The Talmud applies this verse to the Babylonian synagogues and houses of study. More specifically, the Talmud gives the lodging-place of the Divine Presence in Babylon as the famous synagogue Shaf ve-Yativ in Nehardea, traditionally built of stones brought from Zion by the exiles of Jehoaichin, and whose name meant "removed and established." However, some scholars rather tend to see the actual beginnings of the synagogue in the Bible's repeated mention of the assembly of elders before Ezekiel.

Although there is no mention of the synagogue in Ezra and Nehemiah and the post-Exilic prophets, it may be assumed that the returning exiles brought with them the rudiments of that institution to which they had evidently given birth during their exile. Now the establishment of the synagogue implies the evolution of standard forms of service, and significantly, the Talmud ascribes the formulation of the earliest fixed prayers (the *Amidah, Kiddush* and *Havdalah,* as well as public Torah reading) to Ezra

1

and his successors, the Men of the Great Assembly. It is to Moses, however, that the Midrash and other ancient sources ascribe the origin of the synagogue as an institution. Rabbinical literature records no tradition of any contemporary building having been a synagogue during the period of the First Temple, but an ostracon has been unearthed at Elath, which evidently belongs to the sixth century B.C.E., and whose inscription possibly reads *Bet Kenisa bi-Yrushalayim* ("The Synagogue in Jerusalem").

Notwithstanding, there are scholars who assume that the synagogue first emerged a few centuries later in the Hellenistic Diaspora. Describing the Maccabean period in the second century B.C.E., the Books of Maccabees mention public readings from the scrolls of the Torah, as well as the singing of hymns with the refrain "His mercy is good and endureth forever."

Prayer and Sacrifice

Considering likewise the element of prayer, those who date the synagogue back to the First Temple period find indications in Psalms and the Book of Isaiah that sacrifice in the First Temple was accompanied by prayer.

Though there was always a natural tendency to prefer a sacred site such as Shiloh or Gibeon, prayer, unlike sacrifice, could be offered up at any place, as is demonstrated by Biblical instances from Eliezer through to Daniel and Ezra. When praying in Babylon, however, Daniel turned to face Jerusalem. Indeed, at the dedication of the First Temple four centuries earlier, Solomon had said: "Whatever prayer and supplication be made by any man of Thy people Israel—each man knowing the plague of his own heart, and spreading forth his hands toward this house—then hear Thou in heaven Thy dwelling-place." So, too, the Temple's ultimate role as the major place of prayer is described by Isaiah: "Even them will I bring to My holy mountain, and make them joyful in My house of prayer; their burnt-offerings and their sacrifices shall be acceptable upon My altar; for My house shall be called a house of prayer for all peoples."

The Temple

The Temple exercised such a sentimental hold on the Diaspora that on the festivals hugh throngs would converge there in pilgrimage. Inevitably, echoes of its glory were occasionally sounded in the Diaspora.

On the tiny island of Elephantine in the Nile, Jewish mercenaries in the service of the Persians built themselves in the seventh or the sixth century a magnificent temple of stone, cedar and bronze. At Leontopolis, also in Egypt, Onias IV in the second century B.C.E. built a temple, complete with altar and ritual vessels, which was largely patterned after that in Jerusalem. And predictably, it is in the Egyptian Diaspora that archaeology has revealed the remains of the earliest synagogue. In 1902 there was discovered in Schedia, near Alexandria, a marble slab stating that the Jews had dedicated this synagogue to Ptolemy III Euergetes (246–221 B.C.E.) and his queen Berenice. The inscription gives the impression of an institution already long established. The Third Book of the Maccabees mentions the founding of a synagogue at Ptolemais during the reign of his successor, Ptolemy IV, and to the same period belongs a dedicatory inscription found in Lower Egypt granting the synagogue rights of asylum.

The First Century
By the first century C.E., the synagogue emerges from all the literary and archaeological evidence as a well-established and ancient institution, the unrivalled hub of the social and religious life of each community. Early Tiberias was organised like a *polis,* its city council and popular assemblies sometimes meeting in the synagogue. The synagogues of Philo's Alexandria were likewise the centres of communal leadership, and here emerged the notion of separate synagogue-communities within the one city: their civic role is attested by synagogue inscriptions and

Dedicatory stone from the first-century C.E. Theodotus synagogue in the Ophel (City of David), Jerusalem.

tombstones. The Essenes and the Qumran groups also somewhat resembled holy synagogue-communities. The Talmud describes one Alexandrine synagogue (destroyed under Trajan early in the second century) where the members of the various craft guilds sat together, and which was so huge that the voice of the cantor was inaudible to some worshipers, so that flags had to be waved to indicate when they should make the responses. Such organization along vocational lines or according to place of origin, was common in synagogues both before and after the destruction of the Temple. Jerusalem had a Copper-Workers' Synagogue and an Alexandrians' Synagogue, while in the Talmud mention is made of the Babylonian Synagogue in Tiberias, and the Synagogue for Jews of Roman Origin in Mehuza, Babylon.

Ancient Synagogues Outside Erez Israel
Outside Erez Israel, a few hundred other ancient synagogues are known, both from the above sources and from archaeology—in Syria, Phoenicia, Asia Minor, Cyprus, the Balkan Peninsula, Italy, Spain, Gaul, Hungary, Yugoslavia, and North Africa. Inscriptions unearthed to date have told of thirteen synagogues in Rome alone. That this community was organized around its synagogues is suggested by the titles of the communal dignitaries, such as *pater synagogae,* and *archisynagogos,* which is held by some to be equivalent to *rosh ha-knesset,* the popularly elected administrative head of the synagogue body.

The Synagogue at the Temple
In Erez Israel, Josephus and other first-century sources mention synagogues in Dora, Caesarea, Nazareth and Capernaum. The Talmud gives the number of synagogues in Jerusalem at the time of the destruction of the Second Temple as 394, most of them small, according to the archaeological evidence. Most significant of all, however, is the existence of a synagogue on the Temple Mount itself. The scene there on the Day of Atonement as described in the Mishnah shows that there was an organic relationship between synagogue and Temple. "The *hazzan* of the synagogue used to take the Torah scroll and hand it to the chief of

4

the synagogue who handed it to the prefect, who handed it to the high priest, and the high priest received it standing and read it standing," and so on. Similarly, in his vivid account of the festivities during the Sukkot Festival of Water Drawing at the picturesque Spring of Siloam at the foot of the Temple Mount, Joshua ben Hananiah describes the manner in which the day was spent, attending the sacrifices in the Temple alternating with prayer in the synagogue.

In body as in soul, Jerusalem's Temple service was relived by distant worshipers. Just as Onias' Temple in Egypt was architecturally reminiscent of the contemporaneous Second Temple in Jerusalem, so too communal worship outside Jerusalem came to be synchronized with the daily sacrifices on the Temple Mount. While each priestly division with its accompanying levites and Israelite representatives was present during its weekly roster of Temple service, those members of the group who had remained outside Jerusalem gathered in their local synagogues for prayer and fasting, and together read the opening passage of Genesis, on the Creation. It was during this period, more particularly in the last two centuries of the Second Temple, that the Pharisaic teachers emphasized that the Creator, being omnipresent, could be worshiped both in and out of the Temple, and that He was not to be invoked by sacrifices alone. The inception of regional synagogue worship has thus been viewed as one phase in the struggle of the Pharisees to wrest religious prerogatives and control of the Temple from the hands of the aristocratic Sadducees.

The Bet Midrash

Independent of the synagogue, and regarded in the mishnaic period as more holy, was the *bet midrash,* or communal house of study. Because, in the words of Rabbi Joshua ben Levi, this is a place where Torah is exalted whereas in the synagogue prayer is exalted, a synagogue may be converted to a *bet midrash,* being thereby elevated, but not the reverse. Likewise, funds donated for a synagogue may by law be diverted in certain cases to the needs of a house of study or for the support of Torah-scholars, while the contrary is forbidden. Noting the respective natures of these institutions, the Talmud teaches that one who proceeds directly from

Talmud study in a Vilna *bet midrash* before World War II.

the services at the synagogue to the *bet midrash* to study, is deemed worthy of welcoming the Divine Presence; and that whoever enters synagogues and houses of study in this world will be privileged to enter synagogues and houses of study in the world to come. A town which among other things could boast at least ten scholars who freed themselves from work or were supported by the community in order to frequent the synagogue was reckoned a "great city," and thereby eligible for a *sanhedrin* court. Maimonides saw these men as assigned to the synagogue for communal needs, and the traveler Benjamin of Tudela recorded that in twelfth-century Baghdad, the ten heads of the yeshivah "are engaged as their sole occupation in communal affairs; . . . they render decisions on legal and religious questions for all the Jewish inhabitants of the country."

Body and Soul

The community, however, took care to nourish the body as well as the soul. Today's widespread Diaspora practice of reciting *kiddush* in the synagogue, despite the rule that it is recited only at a meal, was justified in its time by the Talmud on the grounds that it was done for the benefit

6

of visitors and wayfarers "who eat, drink, and sleep in the synagogue." That the reference is not to the synagogue proper is clear from the explicit prohibition of eating and drinking in it. Annexes were provided for that purpose, as was the case in a certain Jerusalem synagogue whose inscriptions reveal that one Theodotus son of Vettenos built it in the first century "for the reading of the Torah and teaching of the commandments, and also built the hospice and chambers and water installations for lodging needy strangers."

Order of Service

This triple function of the synagogue—serving prayer, instruction, and communal needs—thus spans its whole history. Likewise, the order of service laid down in the Talmud for daily, Sabbath and festival worship remains unchanged as the fundamental order of service, to which, in the course of the ages, only additions have been made. According to a description in the Mishnah, the Ten Commandments, the *Shema* and the Priestly Benediction were included in a daily service at which the priests and levites officiated and which was held in the Chamber of Hewn Stone, the seat of the *Sanhedrin* Supreme Court. So, too, the above-mentioned Day of Atonement service in which the High Priest participated, included certain Torah readings and benedictions which still figure in the Yom Kippur service today. The sages ascribed to Ezra the institution of regular public Torah readings on Mondays and Thursdays (these being market days) so that people should not go three days without Torah, while those of Sabbaths and festivals were attributed to Moses himself. These readings were supplemented by passages from the prophetic works, which were accompanied, as was the reading from the Torah, by translation into the vernacular, presumably Aramaic and Greek.

After the Temple

When sacrificial service came to an end with the destruction of the Temple in 70 C.E., the synagogue remained unrivalled as the people's religious focus. To be sure, some of the interrupted rituals were forbidden because they belonged to the Temple alone. No synagogue lamp imitates the seven-branched gold candelabrum that once illuminated the approach to the Holy of Holies. On the other hand, many of the customs and rituals of the Temple, such as the *shofar* and the *lulav,* were deliberately transferred to the synagogue. Furthermore, the prohibition of prayer in a place rendered ritually impure by the presence of a corpse, indicates an extension to the synagogue of the Temple ideal of purity, and suggests the likening of prayers to sacrifices. As Hosea had already expressed it during the First Temple period, "We will render for bullocks the offering of our lips." Significantly, too, the word *avodah,* referring to the sacrificial service, was now applied to prayer—"the *avodah* of the heart."

The memory of the old order nevertheless lingered for centuries. Long-buried fragments of engraved wall-tablets show that after the destruction, synagogues perpetuated lists of the priestly families which in happier days had been rostered for weekly duty in the Temple. The colorful procession of these twenty-four priestly watches was still lamented in the sixth century by the liturgical poet Haduta, in later centuries in the hymns of Erez Israel, and in the prayers of the Karaites. As late as the year 1034, Palestine synagogues echoed every Sabbath to the beadle's plaintive query: "Which priestly family is on duty today?" And after the family was named: "May the Merciful One restore the priestly watch to its

Portuguese Jews in Amsterdam on Sukkot. Engraving by B. Picart, c. 1723.

8

Two priests performing the sacrifice outside the Temple. The illuminated word *Avodah* ("service") ultimately denoted divine worship through prayer. From the *Frankfort Mishneh Torah,* Italy, 15th century.

The great synagogue in Florence, designed by a team of architects and completed in 1882. The elaborate decoration is Moorish in style.

place, speedily and in our days, Amen." Such inspired nostalgia surely earns the kind of poetic justice envisaged by Disraeli: "The vineyards of Israel have ceased to exist, but the eternal Law enjoins the children of Israel still to celebrate the vintage. A race that persists in celebrating their vintage although they have no fruits to gather, will regain their vineyards."

Education

From earliest times the synagogue had housed the teachers of the community. In fifth-century Babylonia, for example, each synagogue maintained a *bet sefer* or elementary school, and a *bet talmud* for advanced Torah study. By the Middle Ages the synagogue had virtually merged with the adult *bet midrash,* through its universal practice of group study after the morning and evening prayer-services. Nevertheless, the *bet midrash* maintained its distinctive emphasis: this was where the library was housed, and this was where the rabbi prayed with his students when not required to join communal worship in the synagogue.

In Aggadah

The synagogue's function as a spiritual center substituting for the Temple, applied even to the synagogues outside Erez Israel, which were seen as extra-territorial units in the foreign lands: "In the times to come the synagogues of Babylonia will be transferred to Israel." One sage said that God is to be found in the synagogue, notwithstanding that "the whole world is full of His glory." Another sage interpreted the verse "Lord, Thou hast been our dwelling place" as referring to the synagogue, thus extending the idea.

Attendance at synagogue is encouraged by a great number of talmudic homilies. "A man's prayer is heard only in the synagogue"; "one who has a synagogue in his city and does not attend is called 'a bad neighbor' and brings exile upon himself and his children." Furthermore, "when a person who usually attends synagogue misses a day, God asks after him." One sage attributed the longevity of Babylonian Jews to the fact that they

9

attended synagogue, and another recommended that if one is unable to attend, one should at least pray simultaneously with the synagogue service.

2. THE PULSE OF THE COMMUNITY

In the Middle Ages at least, nearly every Jewish pursuit had a religious flavor. Accordingly, there was practically no activity in the daily life of Jews in medieval and later times which was not reflected in the life of the synagogue. Any person having a private complaint could stand up, demand a hearing, and have the service interrupted until the elders promised him redress. New communal regulations (*takkanot*) and the results of lawsuits were announced, as were articles lost, found, or stolen. Witnesses in pending cases were invited to step forward and, by court order, individuals made public apologies or confessions. Mass meetings too were held there. The most powerful social sanction was the *ḥerem* which, inter alia, prohibited participation in communal worship. In Italy any man intending to leave the community had to announce the fact in synagogue so that any claims against him could be advanced.

On a more personal level, announcements were made whose purpose was to enforce moral and conjugal virtues. In the synagogue mourners were publicly comforted, and the appearance of bridegrooms on the Sabbaths preceding and following the wedding made occasions for congregational rejoicing. Families in centuries past were much involved in each other's affairs, and for gossip or matchmaking or any other plans to be made with a townsman, the natural rendezvous was the synagogue—preferably its courtyard or forecourt. Indoors, too, the women in the gallery and the children everywhere lent the religious service a family atmosphere.

Philanthropy
Philanthropy private and communal was increasingly fostered by the synagogue in medieval and later years. From among the impecunious wayfarers and local beggars huddled on the back bench just inside the syna-

Alms box from a German synagogue (left). Bronze charity box from Reggio, Italy, late 17th century. The inscription *Kuppat ḥevrat kuppat holim* is dated 1830 (center). Charity drum of the Five Shillings Sabbath Charity, London, 19th century, for tickets entitling the poor to meals (right).

gogue door, the homegoing burgher could provide himself with a Sabbath guest who had probably spent the previous night in the hospice attached to the synagogue. According to the needs of the day and the season, it was at the synagogue that the pauper could hear *kiddush,* eat in the *sukkah,* and receive his Purim alms or Passover *maẓẓah* or Sabbath-eve provisions from the community chest.

Alternatively, the synagogue beadle might choose to give him a number *Pletten* of *pletten,* or vouchers, each of which obliged the householder named thereon to provide him with food, drink and lodging for at least three days. Anyone wishing to know just how much a recalcitrant householder could be fined, need only consult one of the surviving communal registers of the last few centuries. Eventually those who refused to cooperate were publicly denounced in the local synagogue, and in some synagogues the names of such offenders were even recorded on a special board. If the penniless one was in need of an interest-free loan, or a dowry for his disadvantaged daughter, he could turn to the appropriate voluntary *ḥevrah,*

11

one of the specialized philanthropic fraternities often affiliated to the local synagogue. When he was ill its members would visit him, or attend to his needs in the local *hekdesh,* the communal infirmary. And after a pogrom it was the same congregants who would ransom him from captivity.

Administration

Whether the ghetto's confining walls were imposed by hostility from without or raised protectively from within, the townsfolk they encompassed increasingly turned for communal leadership to the synagogue. Though central to other communal institutions, it was not necessarily the first to be established in a new settlement, being preceded at times by the burial of a co-religionist in hallowed ground, the organization of sick-visiting, or other forms of mutual aid, each served by its particular *hevrah.* Often, after Temple times, synagogue and community were identical, as regards both the building, and the joint administrative personnel. Thus the law was

"Visiting the Sick," as carried out by members of a synagogue fraternity, Germany, 1748.

12

early codified that members of a community could compel each other to contribute towards erecting a synagogue, and its funds were considered part of the general community funds. When they were distinct, the synagogue authorities were always subservient to the more-encompassing leadership of the community which in the Middle Ages, apart from taxes imposed from outside by the secular authorities, largely governed itself, and maintained its own courts of law. Hence the talmudic injunction against having recourse to non-Jewish courts was reinforced during this period by bans by various rabbinical synods. The court of an autonomous community was strongly bound to the synagogue: its sessions were conducted in or near the synagogue whose rabbis served as judges.

Outside his home, the synagogue was all the medieval Jew had. Little wonder, then, that so much effort was directed by communal leaders and rabbis towards improving the quality of synagogue life by means of *tak-*

Communal Legislation

Die „Freie Vereinigung für die Interessen des orthodoxen Judentums" (Frankfurt am Main) und der „Verein zur Wahrung des gesetzestreuen Judentums in Baden" (Mannheim) geben gemeinsam die Broschüre in neuer Fassung heraus. Sie sind den Herren Rabbinern, die bei der Neuauflage mitgearbeitet und wertvolle Ratschläge erteilt haben, sehr zu Dank verpflichtet.

Kein Minjan!
Eine Gottesdienstordnung für Gemeinden ohne Minjan.

Die kleinen und kleinsten Gemeinden halten an ihrem Ort die Ehrenwache an den jüdischen Einrichtungen, am Gotteshaus, an den Gräbern der Ahnen.

Wertvolle Einzelposten sind sie in der großen Arbeitsgemeinschaft jüdischer Glaubenstreue und selbstloser Pflichterfüllung. Ihnen gebührt der Dank und die Hochschätzung des jüdischen Volkes.

Minjan am Ort zum gemeinschaftlichen Gebet, zur gemeinschaftlichen Erfüllung der Gottesgebote, ist die kleinste Arbeitsgemeinschaft.

Doch selbst an Orten, an denen kein Minjan mehr zustandekommen kann, darf das gemeinsame Gebet nicht fehlen.

Für dieses gemeinsame Gebet in minjanlosen Gemeinden überreichen wir Ihnen diese Anordnung, aus der sich ergibt:

1. Es darf kein Kaddisch gesagt werden, auch nicht Borchu!
2. Die Schmone Esre wird nur leise gebetet, sie darf nicht vom Vorbeter wiederholt werden.
3. Die Sefer Thora darf unter den üblichen Gesängen ausgehoben werden, aber es wird niemand zu ihr aufgerufen. Die Sidra, beziehungsweise der jeweilig vorzulesende Abschnitt, wird ohne Unterbrechung, ohne Bor- und Nach-Borochu verlesen, ebenso die Haftara, der auch kein Segensspruch vorausgeht, oder nachfolgt.
4. Als Ersatz für Kaddisch, Borchu und Kedusche, können im Wochengebet, nach der folgenden Anweilung,
am Werktag: nach Tachanun,
am Schabbos und Festtagen nach der leisen Schmone Esre bzw. nach Hallel, die Einschaltungen Nr. 1, 2 und 3 gesagt werden.
Vor dem Schlußgebet Olenu kann die Einschaltung Nr. 4 gesagt werden.
5. Im Minchagebet kann am Werktag nach Tachanun, am Schabbos nach der leisen Schmone Esre gesagt werden:
Einschaltung Nr. 5 und Nr. 6.
Vor Olenu Einschaltung Nr. 4.
6 Im Maarivgebet kann nach B'hu-rachum Einschaltung Nr. 1 gesagt werden und zwar mit folgenden einleitenden Worten:
זֶה אָנוּ אוֹמְרִים בְּמָקוֹם חַצִּי קַדִּישׁ שֶׁל עַרְבִית
Dann folgt Einschaltung Nr. 7 und Maarivgebet.
Vor Olenu Einschaltung Nr. 4. Am Sabbat-Ausgang wird die Einschaltung Nr. 4 vor וִיהֵן לְךָ gesagt.

Takkanot issued by the German Orthodox rabbinate, establishing the order of service for communities no longer having a *minyan*, 1933.

13

kanot, or regulations. According to a *takkanah* of Rabbenu Gershom a thousand years ago in Germany, although the private owner of a synagogue could choose to close it, he was not permitted to discriminate between prospective worshippers wishing to attend. A ruling by Rabbenu Tam in France in the twelfth century stipulated that the usual fine for bodily assault was to be doubled if the offense was committed in the synagogue.

The right of assembly outside the synagogue was limited by one Italian *takkanah* to six persons, for fear of the dangerous envy of gentile neighbours. Elsewhere in Italy, non-payment of fines was punishable by loss of the right to an *aliyah*—being called to the public reading of the Torah— and by not being counted toward a *minyan,* the statutory quorum of ten for communal prayer. The use of these degradations as judicial sanctions shows what value the medieval Jew placed on those rights. Certain communities fined congregants for unwarranted non-attendance at daily services; once present, they were forbidden to leave the synagogue if they left behind them less than a *minyan.* According to a Castilian synod, the fine paid for smiting or insulting a fellow-congregant in synagogue was to be divided between the Talmud Torah education fund and the poor, or disbursed according to the judges' discretion. The prescribed sum of 200 maravedis did not include damages, being only a penalty for the profanation of the synagogue.

And when the same synod of 1432 laid it down that ten families settling together could be fined for failing to establish a synagogue, perhaps it was because they understood intuitively that it was the light of the synagogue that explains Jewish survival in the Dark Ages. When, with the advent of the "enlightened age," Jews gained admission to the culture and institutions of their respective environments, the functions of the synagogue became more limited to prayer and preaching. But the wheel is come full circle, and a people whose identity and survival have been buffeted as mercilessly by two centuries of emancipation as they had been by two millenia of persecution, has learned in our generation to seek anchorage in a well-tried haven. This rejuvenation of the Diaspora synagogue is taken up in a later chapter.

14

Democracy

Democracy ruled the early synagogue well before it was admitted to other, contemporary institutions: practically anyone could secure a public hearing there, and the services were conducted by members of the congregation. To be sure there was a *rosh knesset* who made the necessary administrative decisions and distributed the honors, but he was elected to that honorary position by popular vote. His decisions were carried out by the *ḥazzan,* who in Temple and talmudic times was the only permanent synagogue official, presumably paid, and who was a beadle rather than a cantor. Although in the Middle Ages only the wealthy could attain positions of authority in the larger synagogues, the humblest umbrella-fixer who could chant the prayers had the opportunity to lead the services, anyone who had a festivity in the family would be called up to the public reading of the Torah, and when called there, everyone read his own portion. The only aristocracy was that of the *kohen* (priest) and *levi* (levite), who were given precedence in the public reading of the Torah, and scholars, who were granted various ceremonial honors.

The ancient counterpart to the modern synagogue president was the *parnas.* Inevitably, there were periods in which the family influence of aspiring office-bearers outweighed their piety. Realizing that power corrupts, the Talmud advises: "You should only appoint as *parnas* over the congregation a man who carries a basket of reptiles on his back, so that if he becomes too arrogant or overbearing, you can tell him: 'Turn around!'" (That is, avoid the risk of appointing a man with an unblemished family history.) Nor was this honorary position considered to be a bed of roses. The Midrash, perhaps with tongue in cheek, teaches: "If a man has sinned, what should he do to atone? If he is accustomed to study, let him intensify his studies; but if he is unlearned, let him seek to be appointed *parnas* over a congregation." Already in antiquity the qualifications for office evidently did not include learning. Indeed, in these ancient references to the questionable humility, ease, and scholarship characterising the position of *parnas,* many a twentieth-century synagogue president will doubtless find a disconcerting modernity.

Leadership

15

To keep pace with the growing range of synagogal activities, new positions were added over the centuries. The *gabbai,* or warden, was originally the official charged with the collection and administration of charities connected with the synagogue, but the term came to cover the functions of the *rosh knesset* when that title fell into disuse. Though these terms were often used indiscriminately, the original order of precedence was *parnas, rosh knesset, gabbai.*

The Ḥazzan

The *ḥazzan* in talmudic times was the communal official who, among other duties, brought out the Torah scrolls for readings, and blew the ram's horn to announce the inauguration of the Sabbath and festivals. He was not regularly required to chant the synagogue service but could do so by request, taking his turn side by side with any other congregant

The *hazzan* of the Amsterdam Ashkenazi community, Jeḥiel Michel, in 1700 (left). A *ḥazzan* with a bird's head, depicted thus in order to avoid disobeying the Second Commandment.   S. Germany, c. 1300 (right).

who might be asked to act as *sheliaḥ ẓibbur,* literally "envoy of the congregation." This function became the prerogative of the *ḥazzan* only in the premedieval period of the *geonim,* with the increasing complexity of the liturgy and a decline in the knowledge of Hebrew, together with a desire to employ music to enhance the beauty of the service. The *ḥazzan,* who traditionally was the guardian of the correctness of the texts, and who selected new prayers, was a natural choice for this task. When the liturgy came to include *piyyutim,* or hymns, it was likewise the *ḥazzan* who would compose and recite them and provide suitable melodies.

During the Middle Ages the professional prayer-leader began to enjoy *Qualifications* longer tenure and higher status, including communal tax exemptions, and his office has since proved to be the most continuous of all synagogue positions. By no means were all *ḥazzanim* eminent rabbis (though this was the case in medieval Northern Europe), but certain qualifications came to be expected. The *ḥazzan* was required to have a pleasant voice and appearance, to be married ("so that his prayer should rise from the very walls of his heart"), to have a beard, to be fully familiar with the liturgy, to be of blameless character, and acceptable in all other respects to the members of the community. Though modified occasionally, these strict requirements have commonly been rigorously enforced on the High Holy Days. Hence, ironically, the growing popularity of his position often made the cantor the community's most controversial official. *Ḥazzanim* vied with each other in displaying their musical virtuosity to the point that the sixteenth-century Code of Jewish Law found it necessary to warn sternly against ostentation, and some cantors were castigated for the needless repetition of words. All in all, services veered from their original direction to become longer, more formal, and more ritualistic.

The Rabbi
It is difficult today to imagine any sort of synagogue without a rabbi. Yet over a hundred Talmudic sages and teachers, whose every recorded word is approached with awe almost two thousand years later, are remembered by their lay vocations as Rabbi Johanan the Cobbler, Isaac Nappaḥa

17

("the smith"), and so on. Their principle was that the Torah had to be taught free of charge. Accordingly, they received no payment for their rabbinic services—deciding legal questions, teaching, and giving spiritual guidance to their communities. They were, however, indirectly subsidised by being given commercial protection. For example, they had the prerogative of selling their wares first. It is probable that a few centuries later certain of the *geonim* were salaried, since the Babylonian gaonate was a full-time occupation. Maimonides, himself a physician, in the twelfth century opposed the institution of the professional rabbi; he preferred the ideal of the scholar who earns his living independently but serves as a communal teacher. So, too, in Yemen, the *mōrī* who served as rabbi, judge and teacher might be paid for teaching, but he more commonly earned his living as a ritual slaughterer or goldsmith.

Through the Middle Ages the position of paid rabbi nonetheless crystallized, but the actual nature of the remuneration is significant. For example, when the rabbinic authority Simeon ben Ẓemah Duran fled from the anti-Jewish riots in Spain in 1391 and arrived in Algiers, the local community wished to appoint him rabbi. He pleaded inability to accept as he was penniless and had to earn his livelihood, as heretofore, from the practice of medicine. In order to enable him to accept the position, a formula was worked out whereby instead of a salary for his services he was to receive compensation for loss of time due to his preoccupation with his rabbinic office. This has remained the basis in Jewish law for a rabbi receiving a salary, even though today it is generally regarded as being in the category of a professional wage, with contracts written between rabbis and their congregations.

Unlike today, however, the *rav* in the Middle Ages and later centuries *Qualifications* was employed not by the synagogue—where he delivered sermons, notably on certain festive Sabbaths—but by the community, which entrusted to him judicial work, social-spiritual leadership, higher education, and *kashrut* arrangements. In addition to his other emoluments, he might receive fees for performing marriages, judging, and the like. His qualification was a document, preferably signed by a renowned rabbi, attesting to

18

his scholarship, his suitability for judging, his character and piety. However, particularly in England, there have been times when the United Synagogue, for example, did not demand that a rabbi acquire a rabbinical diploma. In fact, a student of Jews College still graduates and is qualified to accept a synagogal position on obtaining the minister's diploma, which is less than a rabbinical qualification and carries with it the title of "reverend." Elsewhere, the title most universally used is rabbi, apart from the Sephardi congregations' haham (literally "sage", from the Hebrew *ḥakham*), or *moreh ẓedek* ("teacher of righteousness").

Whatever the rabbi's title in any place or period, it did not vest him with *Functions* priestly or semi-priestly authority or functions. Where legal acumen was required, such as in the preparation and supervision of marriage and divorce proceedings, the rabbi's expertise was of course indispensable. In addition, some rabbis led in prayer and blessed the people, but until modern times this was no more than a matter of personal inclination. Indeed, leading in prayer, blessing the people, and officiating at marriage and burial ceremonies never became an integral part of the conception of rabbinical office until the beginning of the nineteenth century, with the Reform movement. With its progressive rejection of traditionally received *halakhah*, the Reform movement has changed the very concept of rabbi. The Reform rabbi is judge no longer: he has become to a large degree, for the first time in the history of the rabbinate, a priest ordering the prayer service and leading it. In the United States in particular, he is also becoming the social director of his synagogue congregation. The Conservative wing of Judaism, especially in the United States, aims at a stance somewhere between these two positions.

Since the Emancipation especially, the function of rabbis of whatever trend *Governmental* in Judaism has varied somewhat from country to country according to *Interference* local conditions. For example, Prussian legislation at one stage left the rabbi a powerless functionary (after all, even a Jew—the Enlightenment thinker Zunz—had declared the rabbinical office to be altogether dispensable); the Bismarckian Reich on the other hand gave rabbis equal status in some respects with Christian clergy. In certain other German states, government-authorized rabbis of all trends spoke High German and were required to have university degrees in addition to their rabbinic training. In England the rabbi approximated until recently more to the cantor than in any other country. His official title was "minister-preacher," while his colleague was the "minister-reader," both sharing the conducting of services and the reading of the Torah. In France the organizational aspects of the rabbinate were largely determined by the government-established Consistory.

Wherever he worked, however, the modern rabbi has been expected to devote much of his time to pastoral work, establishing a personal bond between himself and his congregants—visiting the sick, officiating at bar-mitzvahs, marriages, funerals, and houses of mourning as a matter of course. He has been expected to take part in all social, educational, and philanthropic activities of the congregation. In addition, especially in the United States, he is often looked to as the spokesman of the Jewish community to the wider community. The influence of the larger non-Jewish denominations, particularly the Protestant Church, has been marked. In England, France and Germany the wearing of canonicals at various periods was obligatory. Until recent times in England it was de rigueur *Pastoral Activities*

Dr. Nelson Glueck, president of the Hebrew Union College, delivering the benediction at the inauguration of President Kennedy, January 20, 1961 (left). Professor Heschel of the J.T.S. in the civil rights march, Alabama, 1965, with Ralph Bunche, Martin Luther King and Ralph D. Abernathy (right).

The chief rabbi of Amsterdam (left), in clerical vestments, 1813, and Rabbi Herman Adler (right), in English clerical garb. 1904.

for the rank-and-file rabbi to wear a clerical collar (commonly known as the "dog-collar"), while at official functions certain chief rabbis donned the gaiters and the silk hat with cockade of the Anglican bishop. Likewise, the garb of the French rabbi in synagogue was identical with that of the Protestant pastor. Recent years, however, have witnessed a considerable departure from these models. In the United States, Canada and England, and in other countries where *yeshivah* education has developed, a return to the old conception of the classic Eastern European rabbi in appearance, outlook, and function is apparent in certain Orthodox circles.

The traditional European rabbi was sometimes assisted by a *dayyan,* a *The Dayyan* judge, who helped constitute a three-man *bet din* tribunal (which often sat in or near the synagogue building) when this was required for a legal decision on certain ritual or civil matters. In London today, the functions of rabbi and judge have been separated, so that *she'elot*—questions on ritual law—are referred by the synagogue rabbi to the *bet din.*

Apart from the rabbis who serve as judges in the religious courts, the functions of the rabbi in modern Israel differ fundamentally from those of his counterpart in any other part of the Jewish world, whether ancient or modern. For one thing, the synagogue in Israel is a place for worship and study, but only occasionally is it a congregational entity with fixed membership. Thus the notion of a personal bond between rabbi and worshiper is not highly developed, and consequently pastoral work is somewhat hampered. Furthermore, marriages are performed by officials of the local religious councils, just as various other activities which are the province of the Diaspora rabbi—involving culture, youth, philanthropy— are in Israel generally undertaken by other agencies. Rabbis, for their part, are often employed by the state as religious functionaries, such as in the inspection of *kashrut* and of *mikva'ot,* or are active in judicial or educational work. Within the synagogues, Israel's rabbis attend to adult education by leading regular study circles, rather than by putting overmuch trust in the benefits of preaching.

The Preacher
From earliest times, preaching to the people has been part of the rabbinic function, the rabbi being both the authoritative scholarly expositor of law and morals, and the moral and spiritual leader of the people. In recent centuries, however, regular preaching was often done by a specialist in the field—the *maggid* or *darshan.* Certain cities had their permanent, salaried *maggid,* but more often the preacher was itinerant, receiving payment for his sermon either from the community authorities or by a collection made after it. This personage was variously held in affection or awe, depending on his eloquence, his wit, his barbs, and his topicality. Surviving regulations of various late medieval European communities insist that before ascending the pulpit any intending preacher was to request permission of the local lay or rabbinic authorities; they evidently held him in the same kind of nervous regard that a high government official today might have for a gifted but unpredictable political columnist. Visiting one town after another, the preacher opened with insistent moral exhortations and rebukes, appealed persuasively for loyalty to tradition, and finally

22

The rabbi preaching in synagogue on *Shabbat Hagadol*, from a *minhagim* book, 1662.

brought solace to the contrite, unlettered multitude by reviving the prophets' promise of a brighter future. Among the memories preserved by today's European expatriates in the New World, tidbits of scriptural interpretation from a favourite *maggid* frequently figure.

The best-loved preacher of all time was undoubtedly Jacob Kranz, the *Jacob Kranz* eighteenth-century *maggid* of Dubno. In order to bring his varied synagogue audiences to the love of their Maker, he drew on the vast resources of Jewish ethical, homiletical, halakhic and kabbalistic material, and simultaneously captivated the hearts of his less scholarly listeners with parables, fables, and epigrams.

During the Middle Ages the tendency developed for the rabbi to preach *Shabbat* only on rare occasions. He usually delivered a halakhic discourse twice in the course of the year, on the Sabbath preceding Passover (*Shabbat ha-Gadol*) and on that between Rosh ha-Shanah and Yom Kippur (*Shabbat Shuvah*). From the beginning of the nineteenth century, however, the rabbi began to assume more and more the function of preacher. In

23

modern times in most synagogues in the western world the rabbi's sermon is an integral part of the synagogue service for Sabbath mornings and even for Friday nights.

In Europe during the Middle Ages most preaching was in Yiddish. With the advent of emancipation, however, serious attempts were made to encourage Jews to use the vernacular, in particular for sermons. In the Austrian Empire, for example, a nineteenth-century decree forbade rabbis to preach in any language other than the vernacular. Originally, such sermons were one of the hallmarks of the Reform movement. In the course of time, however, as rabbis increasingly sought to express Jewish values in a contemporary idiom and in the thought-patterns of the day, preaching in the vernacular became widespread, and is now commonly accepted in the Diaspora, even in the majority of Orthodox synagogues.

Preaching in the Vernacular

קינת ישרון

A Hebrew Dirge,

Chaunted in the Great Synagogue,

ST. JAMES'S PLACE, ALDGATE,

ON THE

Day of the Funeral of her Royal Highness

THE

PRINCESS CHARLOTTE.

By HYMAN HURWITZ,

MASTER OF THE HEBREW ACADEMY

HIGHGATE:

WITH A TRANSLATION IN

ENGLISH VERSE, BY S. T. COLERIDGE, Esq.

London:

Printed by H. Barnett, 2, St. James's Place, Aldgate;

AND SOLD BY T. BOOSEY, 4, OLD BROAD STREET;
LACKINGTON, ALLEN, AND CO. FINSBURY SQUARE;
BRIGGS AND BURTON, 156, LEADENHALL STREET; AND
H. BARNETT, HEBREW BOOKSELLER, 2, ST. JAMES'S
PLACE, ALDGATE.

1817.

Title page of *Kinat Yeshurun,* the first sermon in English, written by Hyman Hurwitz, and translated by the poet Samuel Taylor Coleridge, London, 1817.

24

Wooden synagogue from Horb, Germany, painted in 1735 by Eliezer Sussman. The barrel vault decoration is reminiscent of a tapestry. The walls no longer exist.

(Overleaf) The 14th-century Ark of the Law in the Altneuschul in Prague. The synagogue, one of the oldest in Europe, dates at least to the 12th century.

An indescribable range of preoccupations has characterised different synagogue audiences over the ages, as they have relaxed in their seats waiting for a sermon to begin. Accounts of German Jews martyred in 1096 include an actual sermon publicly delivered to "the first to be slain" and urging them to accept martyrdom. During the period of the Spanish Inquisition, compulsorily-heard Christian evangelist sermons evoked strong reactions from contemporary Jewish preachers. In later centuries Shabbateanism, Ḥasidism, the Enlightenment, Reform, and Zionism were all vehemently argued for and against from the pulpits of Europe. In nineteenth-century America the same applied to the slavery issue. The first sermon to be both delivered and printed in English (London, 1817) was *A Sermon on the Universally Regretted Death of the Most Illustrious Princess Charlotte*. The contemporary sermon frequently addresses itself likewise both to particular problems which agitate the Jewish community— such as the relevance of the Commandments, cultural alienation and ethical conduct—and to wider matters of universal import, including controversial issues of the day.

The Diaspora rabbi-preacher does not have a Hebrew-speaking counter- part of equal standing in Israel. A number of old-time *maggidim* however are active, and in Jerusalem especially, floridly-worded wall posters still announce forthcoming delights.

The Reader of the Law

The ancient practice of reading the Pentateuch publicly was initially carried out in turn by each of the congregants who were so honoured— first a *kohen*, then a levite, followed by other Israelites. In almost all communities, however, with the gradual deterioration of Torah learning among the lay people, not everyone was able to read his own portion. This has therefore become the task of a special synagogue official—the *ba'al keri'ah*, or reader—while the person called to the reading recites the accompanying benedictions. In Yemenite congregations this practice is frowned upon, and each worshiper still takes his turn at publicly reading his own portion when called to the Torah. As one Yemenite put it, "Would *you* wash your hands in preparation for breaking bread, and leave the eating to someone else?"

Another practice kept alive by the Yemenites is the public translation of the Hebrew text of the weekly Scriptural readings, carried out in the ancient period by an official known as the *meturgeman*. A boy is customarily given the honour of standing next to the reader and echoing the Hebrew original, verse by verse, with the Aramaic version of Onkelos.

The Shammash

This was the versatile beadle or sexton who in Europe was retained by the synagogue or some other communal body for a variety of necessary tasks: he was by turns tax-collector, process-server, secretary, messenger, almoner, all-round handyman, or grave-digger. In addition, he sometimes acted as *shulklaper,* knocking his mallet to a distinctive rhythm on window shutters to summon villagers to prayer, to communal meetings, and to funerals. In the days before alarm-clocks, he wakened people with his picturesque sing-song for pre-dawn penitential services. It was also his task to announce the arrival of Sabbath and festivals. In Vilna the *shammash* had to take an oath that he would strictly observe and enforce the communal statutes. Along with the rabbi and the cantor, he was one of the three employees who received a regular salary and a share in the income from fees, partaking as well in the largesse distributed at weddings or other festive occasions.

A carved walnut *shulklaper's* mallet, Hungary, 18th century.

3. IN THE MULTITUDE OF PEOPLE
IS THE KING'S GLORY

From the waters of Babylon to the suburbia of Tel Aviv, every community has found its own way of singing the songs of Zion—new orchestrations of a familiar theme, whose basic motifs remain constant.

The Ḥasidim

Inevitably, spontaneity and devoutness were the price paid for increasing formality. Among those who hankered after the classical "meeting-place"—for this term faithfully translates *bet knesset*—were the *ḥasidim* of the eighteenth century, who in their characteristic *shtibl* ("a little house or room") restored to synagogue practice its old zest. Here, in unpretentious and unembellished premises, fervor and inner feeling were prized over decorous orderliness, the sense of awe was dispelled by joyousness, and the cantor's conscientiously rehearsed arias were replaced by the congregation's artlessly sung hymns and responses.

Ḥasidic joy expressed in dance. Painting by Chenoch Lieberman, 1952.

27

Other salaried officiants and lay officials, including even the *parnas,* likewise found themselves dispensed with. The synagogue was reclaiming its original variegated folk-ethos. Here, from Saturday near sundown until the Sabbath had departed, the ḥasidic *rebbe* presided over the communal *se'udah shlishit,* the mystic twilight meal. His homilies drew their inspiration from kabbalistic as well as conventional rabbinic sources, he was less particular than his fellow-rabbis about fixed times of prayer, and his byword was the Aramaic phrase: "The Merciful One wants 'heart'." He preached from no pulpit, and faced no pews. With its random tables and benches for prayer and study in the *bet midrash* tradition, the *shtibl* interior looked homespun and austere, and thus expressed a revolt, still felt today, against the formalistic and ritualistic attitude of the rabbis of neighboring synagogues.

The Social Structure of the Synagogue

As in the Middle Ages, so too in the modern period the synagogue in Eastern Europe responded to the tastes of the township of which it was the nerve-centre, whether as a house of prayer, study, conversation, or assembly. Scholars did not always rub shoulders with peasants, and may have even preferred to attend a separate *shul.* Within any one synagogue, moreover, the social structure of the *shtetl* ("township") was reflected in the seating arrangements. Along the eastern wall, where the Ark was located, were ranged the most honoured members of the community—the rabbi and the *sheyne Yidn* (the dignified Jews), the men of learning and of substance, as well as men of status, or *yiḥus,* the distinction acquired through family position in the community or through individual achievement in learning, business, or community participation. The seats facing the eastern wall were occupied by the *balebatim,* or burghers, and behind them sat the *proste Yidn* or common Jews—the humble folk, usually assumed to be ignorant and poor. The annual rental value of the seats decreased with their distance from the *mizraḥ,* or eastern wall, until at the western wall were found the beggars and needy strangers, provision for whom was part of the warm and intimate life-style of the *shtetl,* for despite the seating arrangements, life in the *shtetl* was life with people.

28

Key to Plan of the Vilna Synagogue Complex

1. Zydowska (Jews' Street)
2. Iron Gate
3. Strashun Library
4. Great Synagogue, founded 1573
5. Old *Klaus*
6. *Beth midrash* of the Vilna Gaon
7. Klaus of *Kabronim* (Burial Society)
8. Another entrance
9. Iron gate
10. Main entrance
11. Miscellaneous *klausen*
12. Private dwellings
13. Alley
14. The *Schulhof* (synagogue courtyard)
15. Three covered passages leading to *Durchhof*
16. New *Klaus*
17-18. *Klausen* and *ḥadarim*
19. *Klaus* of *Gemillut Ḥesed*
20. *Klaus* of Ḥasidim
21. Private dwellings
22. Site of Vilna Gaon's *sukkah*
23. Workmen's *Klaus*
24. *Durchhof* (other courtyard)
25. Ritual bath *(mikveh)*
26. Painters' *Klaus*

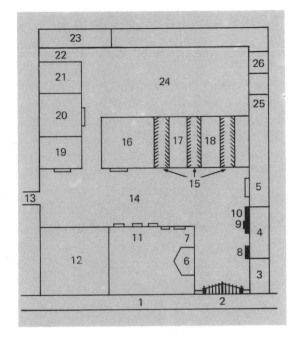

View of the inner courtyard, c. 1916, with three adjoining synagogues (below).

The social groupings in Europe call to mind the great synagogue in Josephus' Alexandria, where the respective guilds sat together for worship. Likewise, the Bessarabian city of Bendery was one of many places to have a Katzovishe Shul (Butchers' Synagogue), other towns had a Schneidershe (Tailors') Shul, while the Hebrew version of the latter serves as the name of the Toferei Begadim Synagogue in modern Istanbul.

In our grandfathers' generation synagogues did not seek pretentiously elo- quent appelations. They usually preferred informally descriptive folk-tags, such as the Corner Shul, Hilltop Shul, a *shul* named after its founder or leading spirit (say Gershon Henich's Ḥevra), the Wooden Shul, the Moyer ("stone") Shul, and an occasional Kalter ("cold") Shul. A synagogue might also be labelled by its innovations, for example the Choir Shul. If a philanthropist endowed a small *bet midrash* where some dozens of youths were "enclosed" with their *rebbe* for the study of Talmud, this institution was accordingly known as a *kloyz* (or *klaus*). The local ḥasidic enclave would typically carry the name of the town where the particular branch of the movement had originated (such as the Belzer Shtibl), while the stronghold of the opponents *(mitnaggedim)* of the ḥasidic movement was often known as the Misnagdisher Shul.

Nowhere is the dilemma of singing the songs of Zion on alien soil better exemplified than in the synagogue names of the New World, such as St John's Wood Synagogue, and even a Christchurch Synagogue. The sense of distance which distressed the founding fathers of many newly-trans-

The shoemakers' prayerhouse in Birzai, northern Lithuania.

30

planted congregations of the first post-European generation, is pathetically expressed in the frequent choice of names such as She'erit Yisra'el ("the remnant of Israel"). Clinging together for group survival in an alien environment, associations of migrants from the same European town or region—*landsmannschaften*—formed the natural kernel of many American congregations. Their European memories understandably left an imprint on the new synagogue names, as did an awareness of their brotherly interdependence. Hence a modest Lower East Side *shtibl* upstairs from the local five and dime, might rejoice in a composite name like Reb Zelig's Anshei Czechstochowa Ahavah ve-Aḥavah Congregation.

The Reform Movement

If Ḥasidism influenced the synagogue in one direction, the Reform movement steered in the opposite direction. The Reform synagogues were elaborate, dignified buildings, lavishly and formally furnished. Whereas the typical ḥasidic *shtibl* was simply an existing building which had been converted to suit its new function, the Reform temple was specifically designed as such. The ark was an impressive edifice dominating the sanctuary, and the *bimah* or reading-desk was moved from the midst of the worshipers to the front of the auditorium. The pulpit was given prominence by the new minister-oriented style of service, the officiants being salaried employees of the congregation. The pews were ordered in straight rows, and there was no separate section for women. The synagogue was relegated to being only a place of prayer, whose atmosphere could be regulated by the adroit manipulation of organ and choir. There can be no doubt that the Reform temples were influenced both in structural style and internal organization by prevailing trends in the various Christian churches. Indeed, the objections of contemporary Orthodox rabbis were largely founded on the prohibition of *ḥukkat ha-goy,* the imitation of gentile practices. The designers of Reform temples focussed on decorum, dignity, and contemporary aesthetic values. These were achieved— but at the cost, to a large degree, of warmth, excitement and spontaneity.

As the Reform Jew was able to find—and did find—his social life outside the synagogue community, there was eventually no need for the other

The Reform synagogue of
Bielefeld, Germany, built in
1904. Note the organ at the
front of the auditorium.

traditional, institutional services of the synagogue, which thus came to
occupy a place in his life analogous to that of the church in the life of
his non-Jewish fellow-citizen. This has especially been the case in Western
Europe and America, with the ever-growing social acceptance of Jews,
of whatever synagogue affiliation.

The earliest evidence of the use of an organ in the synagogue is in Italy in *The Organ*
the 17th century, and the existence of a synagogue organ in Prague in the
late 17th and 18th centuries is indicated by several writers. In the 19th
century the organ was introduced by Reform Judaism into synagogue
services as part of its stress on the aesthetic aspects of Jewish worship.

Of all the liturgical reforms of the century, none has proved to be as
divisive as this. The introduction of an organ into a synagogue was usually
followed by an exodus of the more traditionalist members, who organized
separate services. As the shibboleth of Reform, the organ figured
primarily in Germany and, in the 19th century, in America, though not
in France and Italy. For weekday wedding ceremonies, the organ is
played in some modern Orthodox synagogues. Many American Conservative synagogues also play it on the Sabbath.

In the extensive polemics on the subject, three basic halakhic objections
have been debated: the question of "work" on the Sabbath, the restrictions
on music in general as a sign of mourning for the Temple, and, because
of the organ's close association with Christian worship, the prohibited
"imitation of gentile customs" (*ḥukkat ha-goy*).

The Oriental Synagogue

The centuries have barely affected the synagogues of the Oriental communities, even after their transplanting in modern Israel. The brightly painted walls of the characteristic Oriental synagogue are lined with low benches, which also occupy alcoves, and are often draped with tapestries. Occasionally an ornamented chair, of Moses or Elijah, is attached high up on one wall. The desk from which the Torah is read is in the center, or even placed closer to the west end. Whereas Ashkenazim, or Jews of European origin, refer to it as the *bimah* (or *almemar*), in Sephardi usage it is the *tevah,* and all services are conducted from it, instead of from the accustomed *ammud,* which is the Ashkenazi cantor's lectern to the right of the ark. The ark itself (known as the *heikhal* rather than as the *aron*) is frequently triple, with a smaller closet on either side of the large central one. The Torah scroll, written in a distinctive style of script, is permanently encased in a cylindrical chest of carved wood or engraved metal, sometimes precious. This case is opened and stands erect on the *tevah* while the Torah is publicly read, to a characteristically intricate mode of cantillation.

In some Sephardi communities (those of Spanish and Portuguese origin) the *bet knesset* is known as an *esnoga* rather than a *shul,* and the prayerbook (not a *siddur,* but *tefillot*) is recognizable by its kabbalistic allusions

A Jerusalem Sephardi synagogue, with the *tevah* in the center, and a latticed women's gallery.

and distinctive liturgical rite. In Europe and the United States, the minor differences of this rite often constitute the only feature left to distinguish a Sephardi synagogue from the surrounding Ashkenazi majority.

In the Orient and in Israel, however, Sephardi congregations have often *Spontaneity* succeeded in jealously guarding their distinctive local traditions, without allowing them to fossilize into institutionalization. Suppose an inquisitive Westerner fossicking through an old quarter of Jerusalem pays an un-obtrusive visit to a weekday twilight service in a tiny Persian synagogue. True, the plastic flowers decorating the ark may strike him as unsophisti-cated. But he will immediately sense the spontaneity of the proceedings, epitomized in the person of the congregant or guest whom they have honoured by asking him to act as prayer-leader. As he prepares to repeat the *Amidah* (or *Shemoneh esreh*) prayer as envoy of the congregation, he sometimes reminds himself and them of this relation by symbolically turning to the surrounding worshipers who appointed him, as if to re-assure himself of their assent. He may refresh the immediacy of this contact when intoning the *Shema* prayer. As he chants "In order that your days increase," he may turn and bow towards his elderly country-men who are standing at his right hand, against the *tevah;* " . . . and the days of your sons"—now he turns to invoke this blessing on those watching him from the left. From time to time he may choose to drop the traditional chant and change to a forthright conversational tone in order to emphasize a line which he personally finds to be of especially immediate relevance. At the conclusion of the evening prayer, he turns to his friends, and offers up an informal and obviously spontaneous prayer for their welfare. Grateful to him as the catalyst for a pleasurable group happening, they accompany him to the door with a host of traditional blessings, which he in turn informally reciprocates.

Sephardi synagogues are refreshingly free of spectator worship. At a *The Yemenite* Yemenite service, for example, all those assembled chant most of the *Synagogue* prayers together, loudly and rhythmically. The chants are simpler and perhaps brighter than those of the Ashkenazim, who nevertheless tend to find them monotonous and lacking in warmth. The Jews of Yemen dis-

A Yemenite synagogue in Jerusalem.

dain all cantorial frills, and are so scrupulous in preserving the integrity of their age-old chants, that the pious among them sometimes refrain from serving as *ḥazzanim* out of awe for the responsibility involved. Indeed, when their synagogue music first came to be studied by westerners, one eminent Yemenite scholar objected to recording the time-honoured melodies of certain Yemenite hymns, especially those composed by Shalom Shabazi, because of the sanctity traditionally associated with them.

Some musicologists claim that there are certain rudimentary elements common to the liturgical music of Yemenite Jewry and the Ashkenazim of Poland, and regard this as evidence of a common heritage dating from Temple times. Interestingly, however, while the Yemenites chant the prayers of Rosh ha-Shanah and Yom Kippur according to a distinctive scale of six tones, they do not place any special musical emphasis on the passages whose melodies are the best known highlights of the Ashkenazi service, such as *Kol Nidrei* and *Aleinu*.

This austerity is reflected too in the undecorated whitewashed interior of the *kenis,* as they know their synagogue, which men enter only after removing their shoes, and seat themselves on the rugs which cover the floor. The synagogue commonly bears the name of the philanthropist by whom it was endowed, and whose descendants often exercise their prerogative of serving as *gabbaim.* The synagogue is used exclusively— and frequently—for prayer and study; eating in its precincts is unheard of.

35

Exotic by contrast in the interior of a Bukharan synagogue, such as the Baba Tama in Jerusalem, the walls of which are painted in chequered squares of mustard and olive-green, and hung with deep red tapestries and carpets. Those leading the service sometimes wear a long kaftan-type *djoma,* and certain boys wear a richly-embroidered bar mitzvah cloak modelled on the ceremonial garments of their elders. The *ḥazzan* remains seated in his place for the introductory morning prayers. His art, however, is prized, particularly on festive occasions, such as a circumcision, bar mitzvah or wedding, each of which is marked by its own haunting liturgical melodies, sung in a nasal and somewhat guttural tone.

This synagogue shares many of the earlier-described features characterizing Oriental synagogues in general. In addition, one observes that the high wrought-iron partition around the *bimah* has a gate; in a corner stands a high carved Chair of Elijah for use at circumcisions; diverse lamps and plaques bear the names of departed benefactors. The surnames, like Baibaba and Babayoff, hark from their ancestral Central Asian caravan routes, but the first names are pure Biblical Hebrew. One swarthy fur-hatted worshipper proudly pointed out that each *Sefer Torah* was kept in a proper solid case, sometimes of silver—"not wrapped in some kind of cloth, the way the Ashkenazim do." All in all, with its wide benches covered with home-made upholstery and rugs, its narrow tables and small lecterns standing about in odd places, and the *shammash* serving coffee to the aged participants in the Sabbath afternoon study sessions, the synagogue has a decidedly lived-in atmosphere.

The Theckoobagam synagogue of the "Black" Cochin Jews, reputedly founded in 1625 (left). The Baba Tama Bukharan synagogue in Jerusalem (right).

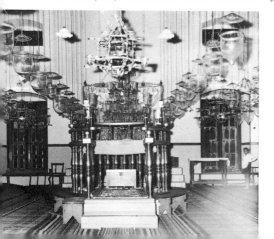 

Sharing the same courtyard are the picturesque houses of prayer of *The Persian* several other small communities, such as the Persian synagogue, where *Synagogue* silver Torah finials decorate the edge of the marble *tevah,* and where after a day's work middle-aged labourers still in their overalls listen to one of their number chanting the daily reading from a book of pious homilies.

The services in the sumptuous synagogues of both "Black" and "White" *Cochin* Cochin Jews in the State of Kerala in South-West India, are conducted in Hebrew. Though most of the women too are able to read the prayers in the original, they are translated in part into the language of the Malabar Coast. Even before marriage, young girls do not enter the synagogue without a head covering. As each festival comes in its season, the women all attend the synagogue wearing clothes of the colour traditionally associated with that festival. The men wear hats to match, and the synagogue hangings for the ark and *bimah* are likewise in harmony. During the Days of Awe, red and white are worn on Rosh ha-Shanah, and white alone on the Day of Atonement. On Sukkot, green is worn to suggest the *lulav*-branch and the foliage covering the *sukkah.* The riotous colours worn together on Simḥat Torah heighten the joy of the communal dancing with the Torah scrolls. To enable the poor to participate as equals in the preparations for the festivals, the synagogue distributes alms to needy families in proportion to their size. The "Black" Cochin Jews have traditionally authorized their synagogue elders to exercise jurisdiction and impose fines, following due warning, in matters such as the desecration of the Sabbath—a rarity—and in civil disputes.

The State of Israel
Being predominantly a Jewish country, many of the functions performed by the synagogue in the Diaspora are carried out in Israel by other agencies, often governmental. The nature of the country also obviates the need to affiliate with a synagogue to express one's Jewish identity. Education, including most religious schooling, is the concern of the state; burial is attended to by independent burial societies; *kashrut* is supervised and arranged by various officials of the Rabbinate, which itself is financed by

37

the government and independent of the synagogue. Thus, paradoxically, the synagogue in Israel is generally used only as a house of prayer and study; most synagogues organize daily and weekly lectures and classes for their congregants. Beyond this, the population, even the religious section of it, finds its expression within other frameworks.

There are, however, indications of a move towards the Diaspora ideal of the multipurpose synagogue. The Iḥud Shivat Ẓiyyon Orthodox congregation in Tel Aviv, for example, is organized around a regular paid-up membership, who have built it into a vigorous community centre complete with weekly *Oneg Shabbat* programs, youth activities, and so on. In the culturally homogeneous semi-ghettoes of certain old-established religious quarters, especially in Jerusalem, the *shul* or *shtibl* has continued to serve as the neighbourhood social center (especially for the menfolk), and the same is true of many rural settlements.

With the ingathering of the exiles, a vast variety of synagogue services *The Army* can be found throughout the country, each Diaspora community bringing to Israel its own colourful customs and manners. Now the beauty of a mosaic or a stained-glass window lies in the fact that a host of colours are seen to advantage in proximity to one another—but at the same time each colour preserves its own hue. However, the multiplicity of synagogal traditions presents a peculiar problem for the army, since it is clearly impossible to establish synagogues suited to the specific customs of diverse communities in every military camp or base. (In the first years of statehood a similar problem had to be faced in the *ma'abarot,* or

Aluf Shlomo Goren, Chief Rabbi of Israel, and former Chief Military Rabbi, carrying a Sefer Torah under a canopy (*ḥuppah*) at the dedication of a new military synagogue.

38

migrant transit camps.) Thus, by force of circumstances, the army serves as a liturgical melting pot, and a uniform type of synagogue is gradually emerging, fostered also by the fact that children from different cultural backgrounds join in prayers and study at religious schools and *yeshivot*. This pattern has been followed by the younger generation in civilian life, and some 300 synagogues of a uniform type have been set up, combining elements from the rituals of the various areas of migration and schools of thought.

An old-new tradition of synagogue usage has had to be forged to meet the novel challenges of army life in a Jewish state. In a country of near-universal conscription, traditional ceremonials too are fitted out in military uniform. Thus, for the full parade which marks the inauguration of a new Torah scroll at an army base, the military rabbinate has laid down a festive form of service in which the *Sefer Torah* itself is borne aloft on a tank, which is bedecked with appropriate biblical inscriptions and military motifs. For field expeditions, the military rabbinate has designed a lightweight ark with a collapsible stand, which houses a small *Sefer Torah,* as well as spare pairs of *tefillin* in a special compartment to replace those lost in battle.

The Soviet Bloc
In the Soviet Union, whose constitution guarantees both "freedom of religious worship" and "anti-religious propaganda," a group of 20 citizens is legally entitled to apply for permission to organize a religious congre-

The former Great Synagogue of Odessa, photographed in 1969, now a sports club.

gation and to acquire a building, or a plot for the erection of a building, to serve as a place of prayer. Those synagogues which still exist in the U.S.S.R. are each a separate society, not belonging to any federative or other country-wide framework. Each of them is administered by a "committee of twenty" (in Soviet usage, *Dvadsatka*), which is responsible to the local authorities concerned with religious affairs that it should not engage in any illicit activity, such as "religious propaganda" (propaganda being explicitly reserved for anti-religious purposes), religious education of children, social welfare work, and the like.

In the early period of the Soviet regime, and particularly during the *The* existence of the Jewish section (Yevsektsiya) of the Communist Party, *Yevsektsiya* when suppression of the Jewish religion was regarded as part of the revolutionary remolding of Jewish society, the closing of synagogues and their transformation into "workers' clubs," cinemas, and so on, became a mass phenomenon. In a matter of a decade or so, innumerable synagogues and other prayerhouses (of the *shtibl* or *minyan*-type) disappeared, and the meeting of Jews, particularly of the younger generation, for organized prayer or Torah study became a hazardous enterprise.

Through sheer tenacity, a few such institutions outlived Stalin. Those *Underground* Lubavitcher (Ḥabad) Ḥasidim who survived Siberia—the price paid for their principles, but in retrospect a badge of honor—tell stories of these underground synagogues and *yeshivot* that constitute a grim latter-day Thousand-and-One Nights. The synagogue in those days meant different things to different people; chameleon-like, it changed its color to survive the developing dangers of its environment.

After World War II, and especially during the regime of Khrushchev (1957–64), a drastic reduction of the remaining number of synagogues took place—from over 400 to about 60–65. Some of them, mainly in Moscow and other larger cities, remained intact in order to serve both as showplaces for visitors from abroad and as centres for the supervision of the remnants of Jewish traditional life by the secret police. At the same time, from behind the scenes, the authorities manipulated the election of the congregation boards by the *Dvadsatka*, so as to infiltrate them by agents or collaborators.

Paradoxically, at the same time in the early 1960s, while synagogues were closed down en masse—their congregants vilified in the press as "speculators" and criminals, and even previously tolerated *minyanim*, congregating in private homes on the High Holidays, brutally dispersed by the police—thousands, and later tens of thousands, of Jewish youth, reawakened to Jewish national consciousness, chose the synagogues, their courtyards and surroundings to demonstrate their Jewish identity by singing and dancing on Simḥat Torah and other holidays. These spontaneous gatherings in and around the few remaining synagogues, which have sometimes been dispersed by the police, have since become a constant feature of Soviet Jewish life, followed closely by diplomatic and press observers from abroad. This has indirectly given them some measure of immunity from persecution.

There are three synagogues in Moscow: the central Great Synagogue at Arkhispova Street and two small ones, in wooden houses, in the suburbs, Maryina Roshcha and Cherkizovo. In addition, a town near Moscow, Malakhovka, also has a synagogue of its own. There is no official connection whatsoever between these three or four synagogues, as no Jewish body of any character in the U.S.S.R. is allowed to exceed its strictly circumscribed local function. Some cities in Georgia, Daghestan, and Uzbekistan also have more than one synagogue—one for the local, non-Ashkenazi community (Georgian Jews, Bukharan Jews or Mountain Jews) and one for the Ashkenazi ("Russian") Jews who settled there, mostly as evacuees or refugees during World War II. There is a conspicuous difference in character between these two categories of synagogues. Whereas the non-Ashkenazi synagogues serve as prayer and meeting houses for the local Jewish population as a whole, comprising entire families and teeming with children and young people (similar to the prayerhouses of their non-Christian neighbors), the Ashkenazi synagogues are, as in the European U.S.S.R., only visited by elderly folk, except sometimes for the demonstrative Simḥat Torah gatherings of the young. **41**

As for all other cities (Leningrad, Kiev, Odessa, Riga, Vilna, Cemauti, Minsk, Novosibirsk, and others), there is only one synagogue in each. In some of them, such as Leningrad, Kiev, or Riga, the prerevolutionary buildings are still in use, and in addition to the large hall, used on holidays, there are also *shtibl*-type prayer rooms attached for weekday and Sabbath services. In others, such as Odessa or Minsk, shabby buildings on the outskirts of the town serve this purpose. There are cities with large Jewish populations, such as Kharkov, in which the last synagogue was closed down some time after World War II and no other allowed to be established. There the militia has systematically persecuted Jews who congregate "illegally" on the High Holidays in private houses for prayer, but on the whole these persecutions have not succeeded in deterring them from repeating this misdemeanor every year anew.

Characteristic of almost all the synagogues in the U.S.S.R. is the heavy atmosphere of fear of the secret police which is generally believed to listen to all conversations and keep a sharp observation of any contact between Soviet citizens and visitors from abroad. One canny visitor pre-arranged a system whereby a local acquaintance signalled to him whether or not the stranger he was interviewing at any particular moment was a "planted" collaborator. In many synagogues, including the central synagogue of Moscow, foreign visitors, including (until 1967) Israel diplomats, are physically segregated from the rest of the congregation by specially erected wooden partitions, the *gabbaim* being responsible for preventing any contact with them.

In other Communist countries in Eastern Europe, the limitations im- *The Rest* posed on the remaining synagogues are less stringent than in the U.S.S.R. *of the Bloc* In most of them countrywide federations of Jewish congregations, or

Festival service at the Choir Synagogue, Bucharest, built in 1866.

religious communities, are allowed to exist and to cater to certain religious needs (baking of *mazzot,* distributing prayer books, and so on) through the synagogues. In Prague the famous Altneuschul is maintained by the authorities as a historical monument, at the same time still serving as a meeting place for prayer. In other Communist capitals possessing modern, imposing synagogue buildings from the 19th or early 20th century, such as Budapest, Bucharest, or Sophia, they are in use and the atmosphere prevailing in them is less suffocating than in the synagogues of the Soviet Union, though the authorities supervise all of them for all kinds of "security" reasons. Most of them also serve as showplaces for visitors from abroad.

4. THOSE WHO MOURN THE DESTRUCTION WILL SURELY REJOICE AT THE REBUILDING

Some time after the Roman destruction, Rabban Gamaliel, Rabbi Eleazar, Rabbi Azariah, Rabbi Joshua and Rabbi Akiva were making their way up to Jerusalem. As they cleared the summit of Mt. Scopus, the desolate sight of the Holy City met their eyes, and they rent their garments. Approaching the Temple Mount they saw a jackal roaming through the ruins of the Holy of Holies. Four scholars wept; Rabbi Akiva alone radiated with joy. They asked him, "Why are you joyful?" Whereupon he asked them, "And why do you weep?" They answered: "In the very sanctuary which was permitted to the High Priest alone, jackals now roam—then shall we not weep?"

Replied Rabbi Akkiva; "And for that very reason I laugh . . . In the Book of Micah it is written, 'Therefore shall Zion for your sake be plowed up like a field.' In the Book of Zechariah it is written, 'Old men and old women shall yet sit in the broad places of Jerusalem.' Until the first prophecy was fulfilled, I may have doubted the truth of the second. Now that the first prophecy has indeed been fulfilled, we may depend without a doubt that the second will also come true!"

—From the Talmud

Ancient Times

For over fifteen hundred years razed synagogues have typified the fortunes of the world's Jewish communities, especially in Christian countries. In the Roman Empire, during the fourth century, Theodosius the Great was frequently obliged to check the excessive zeal of the Christians, who burnt and plundered synagogues or transformed them into churches. Theodosius II, however, expressly forbade the Jews to build new synagogues; and when early in the fifth century the Christians of Antiochia seized certain Jewish places of worship, the emperor, although he at first commanded their restoration, was later persuaded by St. Simeon Stylites to revoke the edict. Pope Gregory the Great at the end of the sixth century was noted for his justice toward the Jews; yet he was unable to restore the synagogues that had been taken from them at Palermo by Bishop Victor and dedicated as churches, although he obliged the bishop to pay for them.

The Middle Ages

The epoch of the Crusaders was initiated by "the liberation of Jerusalem," when the victorious Crusaders in 1099 drove the Jews into a synagogue, and there cremated them. In contrast to this treatment, the Mongols appear benign. When in 1260 they invaded Syria amidst a general massacre, the great synagogue in Aleppo whither the Jews had fled in search of a haven, was left untouched. In France, Philip Augustus commanded in his edict of expulsion, dated 1181, that the synagogues should be transformed into churches, and at the coronation of King Richard I eight years later the synagogues of London were destroyed by the Crusaders. When Philip the Fair expelled the Jews from France, in 1307, the synagogues were either sold or given away, one of those in Paris being presented by the king to his coachman; Louis X restored them when the Jews were recalled in 1315. At the time of the Black Death (1349) the entire community of Vienna sought death in the synagogue in order to escape persecution. In 1473 the Jews were expelled from Mayence and their synagogue dedicated to Christian worship. In 1492 all the Jews were expelled from Spain, their synagogues were turned into churches and convents, and the magnificent synagogue at Toledo, built in the fourteenth century by the statesman

44

A former synagogue in Toledo, Spain, built in the 13th century, and converted into the church of Santa Maria la Blanca.

Samuel Abulafia, became the Church de Nuestra Señora de San Benita (or del Transito), still existing as a monument to the former splendor of the Golden Age of Jewish culture in Spain.

When the Jews of Ratisbon were expelled in 1519, their synagogue, which was built of firestone, was demolished by the citizens (even the nobles and the bishop taking part in the work of destruction), and a church was erected on the site. The intention of Ferdinand I of Austria to transform the synagogues of Prague into churches (1557) was not executed, and it was reserved for Leopold I, another member of the House of Hapsburg, to issue the last general order to this effect recorded in history. When the Jews were expelled from Vienna, in 1670, a church was built on the site of their demolished synagogue.

Mohammedan Lands
These episodes in the history of the synagogue in Christian countries have had very few parallels in Mohammedan lands, although the rule of Islam

also began with an edict against the synagogue. It was decreed in the Covenant of Omar in the seventh century that in those countries which should be conquered no new synagogues might be built, nor old ones repaired. The Calif Al-Mutawakkil confirmed this decree in the ninth century, and commanded that all synagogues be transformed into mosques. The Egyptian calif Al-Ḥakim (d. 1020) also destroyed synagogues, and many were razed in Africa and Spain after 1140 by the fury of the Almohades. The great synagogue of Jerusalem was destroyed in 1473, although the Jews were soon permitted to rebuild it.

The conversion of synagogues into mosques has proceeded in various countries over the years. In 1972, on the occasion of the tenth anniversary of Algeria's independence, the government announced that the synagogue of Oran, reputedly the most beautiful in North Africa, had been confiscated and converted into a mosque.

The Holocaust

The desecration of synagogues and Jewish cemeteries during World War II by the Germans and their collaborators was a carefully planned operation, executed with utmost thoroughness. It was accompanied not only by vandalism and looting, but by cruelty and malice. In many cases Jews were ordered to burn down their houses of worship, while those who refused to obey were punished. "Fire Brigades" were formed in some Polish towns, their task being to set fire to synagogues and religious articles, and sometimes even to worshipers, who were forced inside the building to be burned alive.

It is impossible to ascertain the vast number of art and religious treasures *Statistics and* destroyed or stolen by the Nazis and their fellow travelers and collaborators *Documentation* in the non-Jewish population. Synagogues were destroyed in thousands of communities in Eastern Europe, in the large Jewish settlements in Poland, Lithuania, Latvia and Estonia, the Ukraine, Belorussia and such Central European countries as Germany, Austria, Czechoslovakia, and the Balkans. The religious art treasures of these synagogues ran into hundreds of thousands of items, for every synagogue was virtually a repository of ritual and traditional objects. These included Torah scrolls, Torah mantles, Torah shields and pointers, and Holy Arks, often made of carved wood or stone, with their curtains; there were also Chairs of Elijah, chandeliers, candlesticks, prayer books and *megillot*. The comparatively sparse documentary evidence on the destruction to be found in various archives includes actual destruction orders, the names of those who issued and executed them, and the dates of destruction.

The first attempts to describe the extent of this destruction were made during the war by eyewitnesses, such as Emmanuel Ringelblum and Rabbi Simon Huberband. The former organized "Oneg Shabbat"—the code

The Oranienburgerstrasse synagogue, Berlin, on *Kristallnacht*, November 10, 1938 (left). A former Cracow synagogue, now the studio of the Artists' Cooperative (right). Note the tablets of the law on the wall.

name for the secret documentation work of the Warsaw Jewish underground movement—while the latter listed the destruction of Polish synagogues and Jewish cemeteries. According to data in the Yad Vashem archives, the deportation and liquidation of the Jewish population of Europe was accompanied by the destruction of 33,914 Jewish communities, of which a few thousand were in Poland. It is estimated that 98% of movable Jewish art treasures in Poland, which had been preserved in synagogues or art collections, disappeared during the war. The first official attempt to list the losses in the domain of ritual art objects throughout Poland was made by the Polish Ministry of Culture and Art in a series of publications of the Claims and Reparations Office. A few of the synagogues in Poland have been restored and converted by the authorities into libraries, museums, movie theaters and cultural centers, or have become cooperative grain stores. The architecturally interesting wooden synagogues of Poland were all destroyed by the Germans. Testimony on the destruction of synagogues in Germany and Austria, especially with regard to *Kristallnacht* (1938) was given at the Eichmann trial. On that night, about 280 synagogues were destroyed and burned in Germany alone. Of the 23 Viennese synagogues that had existed before the *Anschluss,* the only remaining one was restored in 1964, and two *battei midrash* were left. The monetary value of 56 synagogues destroyed in Austria on November 10, 1938, alone, is estimated at 5,000,000 dollars.

The Old City of Jerusalem
The Jewish Quarter until recently boasted 58 synagogues which had served the Sephardi and Ashkenazi communities for different periods since the thirteenth century. Then, during the Israel War of Independence of 1948, the Quarter was besieged, and after a prolonged, hopeless but heroic stand, its inhabitants were driven out. During the period of Jordanian rule, contrary to all United Nations armistice agreements, Jews were prohibited from worshiping at the Western Wall, and Arab Legionaries systematically destroyed the Quarter, which for nineteen years lay desolate. The Karaite synagogue which had stood since the tenth century, surviving even the Crusaders, now too succumbed. To tell the stirring history of

most of these razed synagogues there remains nothing but a charred pavement—mute evidence, which will here be supplemented by a paragraph on some of the best known among them.

The renowned Bible commentator Naḥmanides (Rabbi Moshe ben Naḥman—known as Ramban) arrived in the Holy Land from Spain in 1267. When he beheld Jerusalem, still dazed in the wake of the Crusaders, he recalled the prophets' predictions, so literally fulfilled, and rent his garments. The Jewish community consisted of only two cloth-dyers. In a letter to his son Abraham, he described "a ruined building with a beautiful dome supported by marble columns; and we took it as a synagogue, for the city is ownerless, and whoever wishes to take possession of some part of the ruins, may do so." Hearing of such a luminary in Jerusalem, scholars and others flocked there from as far afield as Aleppo and the Euphrates— and the Jewish community was restored to life. *The Ramban Synagogue*

Sephardi and Ashkenazi Jews worshipped together in the Ramban Synagogue until 1585, when the Mufti of Jerusalem turned it into a mosque. Thereupon the Ashkenazim built a new Ramban Synagogue on an adjoining lot. Since the Six-Day War of 1967, the remains of the original synagogue have been excavated and rededicated—exactly 700 years after the initial founding by the Ramban himself. Visitors to the site can read for themselves the text of his letter to his son, on a bronze plaque affixed to the wall.

The Ramban synagogue in Jerusalem. Excavations are still in progress.

49

To offset the confiscation of the Ramban synagogue by the Mufti, the *The Yohanah* Sephardi congregation in 1586 built this synagogue, which also served the *ben Zakkai* needs of the Jews who had fled from the Spanish Inquisition. In fact *Synagogue* it is a complex of four quaint synagogues, each with its own history and folklore. The main synagogue is said to stand on the site where the talmudic sage Yohanan ben Zakkai prayed at the time of the Roman conquest of Jerusalem in 70 C.E. The Sephardi chief rabbis were here inducted into the office of Rishon le-Ziyyon before 1948. The tastefully-restored interior (completed in 1972) incorporates contemporary materials, but otherwise echoes its original plan, including the carved stone details of the triple-arched ark, remnants of which were found lying about after its destruction. In 1948, this was the Old City's last haven.

The adjoining Prophet Elijah Synagogue is associated with a tradition that here the prophet will herald the arrival of the Messiah. The Istanbuli

The Yohanan ben Zakkai synagogue before 1948 (left), and the Istanbuli (right) in a 19th-century engraving.

The Ḥurva (left) before 1948, and (right) in 1967, after the Jordanian Occupation.

Synagogue in the same compound was where the Jewish Quarter's tradesmen used to congregate on Sabbath afternoons to listen to itinerant preachers or to hear readings from a Spanish anthology of laws and edifying parables. It was kept clean by women who volunteered to wash the floors by drawing water from the well in the middle of the synagogue. Old Jerusalemites remember the Istanbuli as a hive of activity at all hours— the Sephardi equivalent of an East European *shtibl,* with ad hoc services starting one after another.

The largest synagogue of the Ashkenazi community was built by members *The Ḥurva* of the Sassoon and Rothschild families for the Polish followers of Rabbi *Synagogue* Yehudah he-Ḥasid who settled in Jerusalem in 1700. When Arabs molested the construction workers, and Rabbi Yehudah died, the unfinished building was left looking like a ruin (*ḥurva* in Hebrew), and nicknamed accordingly. **51**

Completed eventually in 1864, it was a grand edifice, its ornately-painted walls in the shape of four arches meeting to form a lofty dome from which hung an elaborate candelabrum. Though surviving a mere four-score years, it lived through memorable moments in the history of Erez Israel.

In 1920 Sir Herbert Samuel, as first British High Commissioner for Palestine, visited the Ḥurva, and of course was given the traditional Sabbath morning honor of being called to chant the *Haftorah,* the reading from the Prophets. True, the British Mandate was far from being a Jewish regime—but at least the foreign government was represented in the City of David by a Jew. So when during the benedictions following the prophetic promises he raised his voice in the prayer that "On David's throne may no alien sit, and no others ever more inherit his glory"—all those assembled burst into tears. They were not sitting by the waters of Babylon; indeed, they were standing literally on Mt. Zion—yet they wept when they remembered the Zion that once was, and that is yet to be rebuilt.

In 1943, as news of the events of Nazi Europe reached the Jerusalem community, the Hurva Synagogue was the natural meeting place for the unique assemblage of all of Erez Israel's most venerated saints and scholars, who joined there in a day of fasting and supplication.

Supported by an octagonal base of pink Italian marble, stood the synagogue's majestic *bimah.* Here the Ashkenazi chief rabbis A. I. Kook and I. Herzog were inducted into office in 1921 and 1937 respectively. All that is left of that edifice is half of the marble base, and three chipped steps.

> "My memory is aroused and my heart is sore
> When I see every town on its mount, as before,
> While the city of God, the jewel of yore,
> Lies despoiled—yet not in despair."

The Ḥabad Synagogue

These lines, written in Hebrew by Amittai ben Shephatiah of the tenth century in Italy, have been incorporated in the liturgy of the Day of Atonement as part of the concluding *Ne'ilah* service. Never in history could they have been more meaningful than they were to those men who in 1967 chose to spend Yom Kippur in the first *shul* to be rededicated in the Old City—the Ḥabad Synagogue. It was built last century by ḥasidim who were encouraged to go on *aliyah* by their *rebbe,* the *Ẓemaḥ Ẓedek.* During the nineteen years of Jordanian occupation, its ark and other furnishings were destroyed. The synagogue itself was converted into soldiers' latrines. Immediately after the Six-Day War, recalling Moshe ben Naḥman and the resurrection of Jerusalem in 1267, a fearless ḥasid, Reb Moshe by name, followed in the footsteps of his namesake exactly 700 years before, entered the Old City alone, and cleansed and refurbished the synagogue until it was again fit for worship. The President of the State of Israel, Mr. Zalman Shazar, made his way on foot through dank and ruined alleys in order to join in the first prayer service in this synagogue, and thus gave gracious expression to the centrality of the Old City's changing fortunes in the hearts of Israeli and Diaspora Jewry alike.

5. OLD WINE IN NEW VESSELS

As we have seen, the synagogue developed from being a house of prayer into the center of the Jewish community and then, with the emancipation, it reverted to its role as house of prayer. In the twentieth century it is again taking up its central role in Jewish society, particularly in the United States and Western Europe.

The Early Years
After the mass migration of Jews from Eastern Europe to the United States at the end of the nineteenth century and beginning of the twentieth (some 2½ million Jews arrived in the U.S. between 1880 and 1914) they established synagogues mainly on a *landsmannschaft* basis; people originating from the same locality in the "old country" tended to live in close proximity to each other and set up their own synagogue, often with the original rabbi and *ḥazzan* who had also immigrated. Slowly, as their

economic position improved and they became more acculturized they moved out of their self-chosen ghettoes into other, usually pleasanter sections of town. This is particularly true of the second generation, and the *landsmannschaft*-type affiliation collapsed. Synagogues were established in the new areas of settlement according to the needs of the inhabitants, particularly the need for some organized Jewish education for the children. All the trends in Judaism, Orthodox, Conservative and Reform, took part in this activity and indeed there was often fierce competition between them; the more members a synagogue has the more viable it is financially and, to some extent, the rabbi's success was measured by the number of congregants he could attract. The aesthetic standards of the synagogues rose together with the living standards of the congregants, and magnificent, costly edifices were erected, often designed by famous architects. The Jews were determined to have their synagogues if not the highest buildings in town, then at least among the most beautiful.

Assimilation
In their new environment, attending the same schools and colleges as their non-Jewish neighbors and enjoying equal civil rights, the danger of assimilation for the Jews became far more serious than it had been for centuries. Intermarriage into the general community, perhaps the best measuring-rod of assimilation, rose to hitherto unknown heights and Jewish leaders, both religious and secular, began to fear for the fate of Judaism in the New World.

The Jewish Center
One of the leading figures in the Conservative movement who later created and led its most liberal wing, Reconstructionism, was Mordecai Kaplan. He formulated the concept of the "Synagogue Center," a concept which greatly influenced the synagogue in all the various trends in Judaism in the whole western world. He felt that the synagogue, if it were to continue to play its role in Jewish life, had to be more than a prayerhouse and, in view of the disintegration of traditional Jewish values in the U.S., more than a house of study. He therefore advocated that the synagogue become an all-

54

embracing center of Jewish social and cultural activity with the aim that the Jew spend a great deal, if not most, of his leisure time within the confines of the synagogue building. Such a building would no longer be a synagogue but a "Jewish Center" and "instead of the primary purpose of congregation organizations being worship, it should be social togetherness ... The history of the synagogue ... is a striking illustration of the importance of creating new social agencies when new conditions arise that threaten the life of a people or of its religion."

Program According to Kaplan, the Jewish center should contain a swimming pool, gymnasium, library, club rooms, public hall, and classrooms in addition to facilities for worship. It should provide professional club leaders to supervise groups for adults as well as children involving all the activities in which the membership is likely to be interested, and not only of a Jewish nature, but also such activities as photography, drama, music, and sport. Although most congregations have been unable to provide this comprehensive program, both because of financial inadequacies and the fact that other existing organizations such as the YMHA already provide some of them, it has remained the ideal for which to aim, with the result varying from synagogue to synagogue.

Affiliated Clubs In addition, various organisations are commonly founded around the synagogue and affiliated to it. There is usually a sisterhood for the women, and a men's club; these groups are involved in all sorts of

The swimming pool of the Worcester, Mass. community center (left). A rehearsal for bar mitzvah children in a Richland, Washington synagogue (right).

philanthropic activities. Clubs for children and teenagers are very common, as are groups for young married couples. As the function of the synagogue has widened, so has that of its chief functionary, the rabbi. In addition to being the teacher, religious guide and preacher of the congregation he has now assumed the role, to a greater or lesser degree, of social counsellor, overseeing and guiding all the varied activities which the synagogue now provides.

Besides the traditional "special Sabbaths" new ones have been created. *Special Sabbaths* There are the Men's Club Sabbath, the Sisterhood Sabbath, the Youth Club Sabbath. Special occasions are marked in the synagogue. The bar mitzvah celebration has become much more formal and ceremonious than hitherto, and the bat mitzvah ceremony for girls has become common. Some synagogues, particularly Reform, have an annual confirmation ceremony for all the girls who have "come of age."

The synagogue has always been the center of Jewish education, particu- *Education* larly for children. In the new environment many synagogues sponsor all-day schools in which the usual secular curriculum is taught as well as the traditional Jewish religious studies. Often the synagogue is a complex of buildings one of which is a modern, well-equipped school with good sports and recreational facilities.

In order to house the numbers that attend synagogue on special occasions *Microphones* the main sanctuary is usually very large; for weekday services a small chapel or *bet midrash* is provided. The size of the main sanctuary creates acoustic problems which are solved in Reform and Conservative synagogues by the use of an amplification system. In recent years the use of microphones of a prescribed type has been given a restricted sanction by a few Orthodox rabbis. The question of their halakhic permissibility has been the subject of many modern responsa.

The synagogue is fullest on three days of the year, the two days of Rosh *Expanding* ha-Shanah (the New Year festival) and Yom Kippur (the Day of Atone- *Synagogues* ment). Very few synagogues are big enough to seat all those who attend, and "parallel" or "overflow" services are held in other rooms in the

56

synagogue building or in nearby halls. This practice requires the employment of more staff for the holiday period; each service requires a rabbi and *hazzan* at least. Many modern congregations obviate this by having the main sanctuary of the synagogue adjacent to the synagogue hall and separated from it by a movable wall. For the High Holidays the wall is removed and thus the synagogue space is greatly enlarged.

Synagogue Organizations

A modern phenomenon has been the organization of synagogues of a like type into a synagogue union. In the past, particularly in Central and Eastern Europe, there were periods in which *kehillot* were so organized, but the organization of actual synagogues is comparatively new. The reason for this "unionization" is the fact that an individual synagogue is unable by itself to provide adequate educational and religious facilities, whereas several synagogues together have enough resources to take care of such things as religious education, *kashrut* and burial. Another reason may be the influence of the Christian churches, which are affiliated to their respective church organizations.

The United Synagogue of England has a chief rabbi, a *bet din,* a *kashrut* *England* division, and a religious educational framework. Salaries of the officials in its constituent synagogues are scaled and candidates for such positions are required to obtain a certificate of competence from the chief rabbi. The rabbinical school, Jews' College, functions under its auspices and the chief rabbi, ex officio, is its president. There are two other Orthodox synagogue organizations: the Federation of Synagogues, and, more to the right, the Union of Orthodox Hebrew Congregations (Adath Yisroel). Both of these organizations provide services for their constituents, though

The main hall of the Lubavitch School, London, also designed as a gymnasium, being converted into a synagogue by means of a collapsible *bimah.*

not on the same scale as the United Synagogue. The Reform synagogues of England are also organized, as are the Liberal synagogues.

In the United States there is a Union of Orthodox Jewish Congregations, a United Synagogue (Conservative) and a Union of American Hebrew Congregations (Reform); each of these has its own rabbinical school. Besides the above, the U.S. has several other synagogue organizations, varying in their degrees of Orthodoxy. A recent development has been the creation of international synagogue organizations. The Conservative movement is organized into a World Council of Synagogues, which embraces Conservative-type synagogues in several countries and which meets every two years to discuss problems of mutual interest; there is also considerable movement of Conservative rabbis to synagogues in other countries due to the existence of this organization. *The United States*

In Israel many Orthodox synagogues are organized into the Union of Synagogues in Israel, and the Conservative and Reform synagogues have their own organizations. Most other countries with a sizable Jewish population have similar organizations to those described above. *The State of Israel*

Statistics
In trying to arrive at some estimate of the number of synagogues in existence one is faced with the problem of definition. Is a group of ten people meeting in somebody's house for the purpose of praying to be considered a synagogue? Is a magnificent edifice no longer used to be so considered? Furthermore, the statistics offered by the various synagogue organizations are unreliable, firstly because of the aforementioned problem of definition—by and large the organizations tend to include everything that can be conceivably included—and secondly because a great number of synagogues are not affiliated to any organization.

The figures in the table have been abstracted from *The Jewish Year Book* (1970), *The American Jewish Year Book* (1963–1970), *Communauté,* 15–17 (1961–1967); 20 (1968), and *Comunidades Judias de Latinoamerica* (1968), and should be viewed as approximate. **58**

Country	Estimated number of synagogues	Country	Estimated number of synagogues	Country	Estimated number of synagogues
Afghanistan	1	Germany, East	8	Pakistan	1
†Algeria	5	Germany, West	5	Panama	3
Argentina	99	Gibraltar	4	Paraguay	3
Aruba	1	Great Britain	399	Peru	6
Australia	53	Greece	4	Philippines	1
Austria	10	Guatemala	1	Poland	1
Bahamas	1	Holland	20	Portugal	3
Belgium	19	Hong Kong	1	Rhodesia	8
Bolivia	4	Hungary	30	Rumania	3
Brazil	32	India	27	Singapore	2
Bulgaria	1	Iran	50	South Africa	166
Burma	1	Iraq	3	Spain	3
Canada	169	Ireland, Republic of	8	Sudan	1
Channel Islands	1	††Israel	6,000	Surinam	2
Chile	1	Italy	54	Sweden	10
Colombia	9	Jamaica	1	Switzerland	24
Costa Rica	1	Japan	1	Syria	5
Cuba	1	Kenya	1	Trinidad	1
Curacao	2	Lebanon	2	Tunisia	2
Czechoslovakia	2	Libya	3	Turkey	26
Denmark	2	Luxembourg	3	†††United States	5,500
Dominican Republic	2	Malta	1	Uruguay	8
Ecuador	1	Mexico	14	††††U.S.S.R.	62
Egypt	3	Morocco	50	Venezuela	4
Ethiopia	1	New Zealand	7	Virgin Islands	1
Finland	2	Nicaragua	1	Yugoslavia	2
France	187	Norway	2	Zambia	3

† Figures for Arab countries are estimates according to number of Jews and communities.

†† Ministry for Religious Affairs figure.

††† In 1970 the Conservatives claimed 830, the Reform 698; in 1963 the Orthodox claimed 3,900 in U.S. and Canada.

†††† AJYB estimate; Soviet sources have 97 and Rabbi Lewin of Moscow stated 102.

6. TO EXALT THE HOUSE OF OUR LORD

Synagogues have not always been ideally situated. As early as in talmudic times some were built outside the city, which created a problem of personal safety. Special passages were therefore introduced into the liturgy to lengthen the service so that those who arrived late could finish with the congregation and thus not have to return home alone. One such addition, during the Friday evening service, is the reading of the mishnaic passage *Ba-meh madlikin* which deals with the kindling of the Sabbath-eve lights.

Water

Often synagogues were constructed near bodies of water, as was the case at Capernaum and Caesarea. Josephus too speaks of a custom of Hellenistic Jewish communities "who make their places of worship near the sea." It has been suggested that this custom may have a common origin with the *Tashlikh* ceremony of Rosh ha-Shanah, in which the casting of transgressions into the depths of the sea is a symbol of repentance and forgiveness. Alternatively, the site may have been chosen to obviate the need for a *mikveh*—the immersion bath used for ritual purification.

Height

The law nevertheless prefers that the site should be the highest spot in the city, as was the case in ancient Chorazin, and the synagogue the highest building. Indeed, the talmudic scholar Rav taught that "any city whose

The synagogue of Bedzin, S.E. Poland, destroyed by the Nazis.

60

The Tiferet Israel Synagogue, dedicated in 1865, rising high over the houses of the Jewish Quarter of Jerusalem before the Jordanian Occupation.

roofs are higher than the synagogue will ultimately be destroyed, for it is written 'to exalt the house of our Lord'." In many times and places, however, Jews have been unable to comply with the requirements of this law, for practical reasons and because of restrictive decrees. Hence, in the Middle Ages, Jews made their point by erecting on the roof of the humbled synagogue a pole or rod which rose a little higher than the surrounding buildings. As long as this extension could be considered a "built one" rather than a mere attachment, this method of compliance was deemed legally acceptable.

Orientation

"My heart is in the east
While I am at remotest west."

(Judah Halevi, Spain, twelfth century)

Solomon's inaugural prayer on the centrality of the Temple, and the fact that Daniel prayed facing Jerusalem, are the sources for the requirement that synagogues be oriented toward Jerusalem, and that those in the Holy City itself face the direction of the Temple. This orientation is particularly prescribed by the Talmud for the recitation of the *Amidah* prayer. Since,

61

however, it has not always been possible to orient the building in this direction, it has become acceptable for the synagogue to be planned as close to the ideal direction as circumstances allow.

Interestingly, according to one early source, the Tosefta, it is the entrance to the synagogue that should be on the side of the building facing Jerusalem. Excavations of some early synagogues in the northern part of Israel have in fact revealed that the main entrances are located on the south side, that is, toward Jerusalem. The halakhic codes, however, require that the very opposite be done, because the Holy Ark is placed on the side facing Jerusalem, and it would be unseemly to enter the sanctuary from that side. Furthermore, doors located in the opposite wall would allow the worshipper to bow in the direction of the ark as he entered. This difference in legal views can perhaps be explained by the institution of a fixed ark within the synagogue.

The Vestibule

When possible, it is required that one should pass through a vestibule to the main sanctuary to preclude entering directly from the street. Judah Loew ben Bezalel (the Maharal) of Prague explains that in the anteroom one has an opportunity to shed the thoughts and cares of the outer world before entering the holiness of the inner sanctuary.

Windows

The synagogue must have windows, a requirement stemming from the verse which describes how Daniel prayed by windows facing the direction of Jerusalem. The Talmud warns against praying in a windowless room, and the *halakhah* states that there should be twelve windows, perhaps symbolic of the twelve tribes. This stipulation is rarely fulfilled because of architectural and other problems. Rashi, the French luminary of the eleventh century, commented that windows are required because they allow the supplicant a glimpse of the sky, the sight of which inspires reverence and devotion during prayer. If a wall is built in front of synagogue windows, Jewish Law not only lays down that it is to be demolished, but the usual requirement of its rebuilding at a minimum distance of four cubits (six feet) is insufficient "because the synagogue needs an abundance of light."

Separate Seating

In its description of the festivities held on the second evening of the feast of Sukkot in the court of women in the Temple, the Talmud states that men and women were allotted separate space. From this passage derives the origin of the *mehizah,* the partition screen in synagogues between the space reserved for men and that, generally in the rear or upstairs, for women. Further sources for the separation of the sexes during prayer are to be found in midrashic literature, where it is stated that men and women stood separately when the Israelites assembled at Mt. Sinai to receive the Ten Commandments. Following the Crossing of the Red Sea, Miriam led the women separately to sing the Song of the Sea, the exuberant hymn of triumph and gratitude which had just been sung by Moses and the Children of Israel. This too was taken as an authority for the segregation of the sexes in prayer. Remains of galleries discovered in ancient Palestine synagogues are taken as having served the women worshipers.

Most European synagogues of the Middle Ages had a separate women's *Weibershul* gallery called *weibershul* fenced off by an iron grille or a non-transparent curtain. In synagogues where there was no balcony, the *mehizah* was made of latticework serving as a partition between the seats of the men

"Dedication to the Torah," by Moritz Oppenheim, 1869. Women are seen peeking through the *mehizah* as a father with his year-old son presents a wrapper (see page 103).

63

in front and those of the women in the rear. References to the *meḥizah* in the Middle Ages can be found in the rabbinic responsa literature of that period, where it is stated: "We are permitted on Sabbath to erect the partition-curtain between men and women during the time of the sermon."

The Zoggeren

The problem of womenfolk who were more devout than literate found a novel solution in Eastern Europe. Each women's gallery appointed a pious dowager to read the prayers aloud, and all those assembled repeated them after her, word by word. In the best Yiddish tradition the scholarly one's vocation usually became part of her name, and as a kind of affectionate title of honour she might be known, for example, as Yente di Zoggeren ("Yente the Reciter"). This institution has an interesting architectural corollary, because the problem of designing a women's gallery which would be in the desired degree of contact with the proceedings in the synagogue proper, becomes less urgent when there is a rudimentary separate women's service.

Surprisingly, perhaps even uniquely, the women's gallery at the Paradesi synagogue of the Cochin Jews of India even has a *bimah* of its own. It transpires, however, that this reading table, placed as on a balcony at the front of the women's gallery, is not the focus of a separate women's service, but a facility of the men's synagogue. Whereas on weekdays the Torah scrolls are read at the conventional downstairs *bimah*, on the Sabbath and festivals the voice of the reader resounds from the upstairs *bimah*, the intention being to accentuate the ceremoniousness of the occasion.

Abolition of the Meḥizah

The abolition of the *meḥizah* by the Reform movement in Europe in the early part of the 19th century was strongly opposed by the leading rabbinic authorities in Hungary and Poland, who regarded this innovation as an illicit change, and consequently ruled that any synagogue without a *meḥizah* is unfit for prayer.

In most Conservative synagogues in the United States, the *meḥizah* has been abolished and men and women sit together, or, in some cases, one side of the synagogue is reserved for the men and the other for the

The women's gallery in the Great Synagogue of Sydney, Australia, consecrated in 1878.

women, without an actual partition. In Reform synagogues the segregation of men and women has been entirely abolished, it being argued that the Bible nowhere explicitly commands the separation of men and women during public worship or assemblies. These modern trends have met with vigorous opposition in the last decade on the part of Orthodox Jewry in the United States, which has come to regard the retention of the *meḥiẓah* as a cardinal principle and as a mark of the preservation of the Orthodox character of the synagogue. In several congregations which decided to abolish separate seating the Orthodox minority turned to the civil courts for legal redress and were granted relief by court orders enjoining the synagogue board from changing the status quo, as in the case of Congregation Beth Tefilas Moses of Mount Clemens, Michigan. Similar litigations were dealt with by the state courts in New Orleans, Louisiana and by the Superior Court of Pennsylvania, all of which ruled in favor of the party demanding the retention of the *meḥiẓah*.

In some Orthodox synagogues a modern solution has been found by making the *meḥiẓah* of one-way glass so that the women can see what is happening in the main synagogue without the men being able to see them.

7. BEHOLD THEY HAD DONE IT AS THE LORD HAD COMMANDED

As is to be expected for an institution so central to Judaism, the *halakhah* regulates nearly all the synagogue's manifold aspects: design and location of the building; furnishings and interior design; uses to which the synagogue and its furnishings may be put; and ownership and disposal of the building. In other chapters many of the laws have been recorded with regard to specific issues or objects; here the more general laws and customs will be discussed.

Use of the Synagogue

Although not possessing the same holiness as the Temple, the rabbis *Behavior* have ascribed to the synagogue a holiness patterned after that of the Temple. Accordingly, the Shulḥan Arukh proscribes certain kinds of behavior in the synagogue; for example, frivolity, gossiping, eating, drinking, beautifying oneself, sleeping or napping, entering with an unsheathed knife, or to escape bad weather, or as a short cut, transacting business (other than charity and the redemption of captives), and delivering eulogies (unless for one of the city's great men). One may run when going to synagogue, but on leaving one must walk, in order to indicate reluctance.

Historically, gaming in the synagogue was not uncommon; a sharp con- *Gambling* trast was drawn, however, between the usual forms of gambling, and cases where the primary motive was not personal gain. A multitude of responsa cite instances where the winnings at games of chance were not considered fruits of sin. One statement differentiated between gambling for private gain and that in which the winnings, even if only in part, went to charity. It saw no violation in the latter case and demanded full payment of gambling debts to charity. There were many instances where the rabbis and communities joined in games of chance. One rabbi ruled that he who wins at a lottery should pronounce the blessing *she-heheyanu;* should one win together with a partner, one must also add the blessing *ha-tov ve-ha-metiv.* It seems hardly likely that any blessing should be required if the winnings were considered the rewards of sinful acts. It would thus appear that Jewish law proscribes the professional and compulsive act of gambling; condemns the occasional act of gambling when indulged in for personal gain; while occasional gambling, where all or part of the winnings go to charity, has never aroused condemnation and frequently even has had the approval of Jewish communities.

These observations may have a bearing on the modern controversy over congregationally sponsored bingo and card games organized to raise funds to meet the formidable budgets of synagogues. Jewish history and rabbinic literature show that such methods are not new. Synagogues and communities have indulged in similar games in the past, and the revenues have been used to meet their financial obligations. Rabbis not only did not frown upon such acts but frequently encouraged them. The United Synagogue of America at successive conventions has, however, ruled that bingo is a form of fund-raising not to be permitted by its congregations, the opinion being that it is not in keeping with the spirit of Judaism.

Dirt and rubbish are not permitted to collect in the synagogue, and al- *Cleanliness* though one may enter with one's staff and satchel, it is first required that one clean one's shoes of mud. The upper stories of the building may be used only for purposes which do not violate its spirit as a sanctuary, and it is doubtful whether one may live on top of a synagogue. Even after a synagogue has become a ruin these regulations apply, unless specific conditions were made at the time of construction. These exemptions, however, must never result in the use of the ruin for "a degraded purpose" such as transacting business. If a private home is used as a synagogue, many of these stipulations do not hold.

Holiness of Ceremonial Objects
All objects in the synagogue acquire sanctity by virtue of the sacred purposes which they serve and therefore *halakhah* governs their use. The Shulḥan Arukh specifies that book-cases which have held sacred books, the ark in which the Torah has stood, and the *parokhet* which has hung

in front of the ark are endowed with sanctity, and hence when no long usable must be stored away rather than destroyed.

The holiness of objects is determined by their proximity, in space and use, to the Torah scroll, the most sacred object in the synagogue. The Talmud forbids using synagogue objects in a way which would cause them to decline in sanctity. Thus a discarded ark may not be used to make a chair on which to set the scroll—the chair's holiness being considered less than that of the ark. The reverse order of appropriation, to elevate an object in holiness, is permissible.

Ownership and Disposal

The synagogue is owned by the congregation and those who contributed toward its construction. The concept of synagogue ownership differs in a small village and in a large town or city. In the former it is assumed that there are no donations from outsiders and therefore a decision of the congregation or their representatives—the "seven good men" of the town—is sufficient in order to sell the synagogue building. But in the

A *parokhet* (left) from Frankfort, 1731, embroidered with the donors' names, and (right) a dedicatory inscription dated 1823 in the Casale Monferrato synagogue, in Italy.

city the sale of the building is more difficult, it being unclear whether strangers contributed to the building, and selling without their consent would deprive them of what is, in part, rightfully theirs. *Halakhah* suggests ways to resolve this difficulty, such as selecting, at the time of construction, either a specific rabbi whose decision would be accepted by all, or reserving this power to whichever rabbi is serving when the decision must be made.

It is forbidden to demolish a synagogue until another is provided to take its place, to preclude the possibility of a congregation being without a synagogue should the construction of the second building be delayed or interrupted. In the event that the first synagogue is in such a state of disrepair that it is in danger of collapsing, however, it is permitted to demolish the building and to begin construction of the new one immediately.

If a congregation decides to divide into two, the sacred objects must be divided between the two new congregations in proportion to their membership. The rabbis, however, debated whether women and children are to be included when calculating the proportions. Those who donate articles to the synagogue have the right to have their names inscribed on them. Such inscriptions are permitted only for the persons who actually give money or contribute personal service for synagogue construction, maintenance, or beautification. Synagogue officers during whose term alteration or expansion is undertaken or completed are forbidden to inscribe their names on the improvements or additions.

Weddings in the Synagogue

Among Sephardim the custom has been to perform the wedding ceremony in the synagogue; Ashkenazim, however, traditionally hold the ceremony out of doors, usually in the synagogue courtyard. Since wedding ceremonies used to take place at night, having the *ḥuppah* in the open symbolized the blessing "and you shall be like the stars of heaven." Indeed, many Ashkenazi authorities specifically forbid performing the marriage ceremony within the synagogue because the frivolity usual at such occasions is far from the dignity and decorum required in the synagogue.

In recent times, however, it has become common even among Ashkenazim, particularly in the western world, to celebrate the wedding ceremony in the synagogue, and special facilities are incorporated in many modern synagogues for this purpose. Usually there is some permanent arrangement for the erection of the marriage-canopy, either on the *bimah* or on the platform in front of the ark. Furthermore many synagogues have a "bride's room," where the bride can make her last-minute preparations, and where the couple retire for the short period of privacy that is part of the Orthodox wedding ceremony.

Festivals in the Synagogue

Besides the various changes in the liturgy that accompany the festivals, for some of them the synagogue takes on a different atmosphere in keeping with the nature of the festival. Many synagogues use a different *parokhet*

Festivals in the synagogue. At left, Purim at Kibbutz Yavneh; lower left, Simḥat Torah procession at Leghorn (painting by S. A. Hart, 1841); lower right, "Shavuot," by M. Oppenheim, 1880.

for each festival with ornamentation appropriate to the particular day. This is also the usage with the Torah mantle. During the High Holyday period they are usually white, as are the canonicals of the officiating ministers. For Tish'ah be-Av, the day of national mourning for the destruction of the Temple, the *parokhet* is removed and the ark is left stark and bare. For that day the synagogue lighting is subdued and the congregants sit on the floor or on low benches rather than in the normal pews. The joy of Shavuot, the festival commemorating the revelation at Sinai, is reflected in the synagogue decorations consisting of flowers and plants, symbolic of the mountain on which the Torah was given.

On occasion the decorous dignity the synagogue demands is relaxed. On Simḥat Torah, happy circuits are made around the *bimah* with the Torah scrolls, the dancing congregants taking turns at the honor of holding a scroll. On Purim, the quiet which attends the reading of the Scroll of Esther is shattered every time the wicked Haman's name is read; children—and grown-ups—twirl rattles or shoot off cap-guns to celebrate his well-deserved downfall.

8. HEAVEN AND THE HEAVEN OF HEAVENS CANNOT CONTAIN THEE

In contrast to the Temple, in which the ritual was conducted inside the sanctuary by the priests only, while the other worshipers stood at a distance, the synagogue was a new type of religious building. It was based on the participation of all those assembled in a collective act of worship conducted around a focus inside the building, with space, seating and lighting suited to the public reading of the Torah. Hence the design of the synagogue was not found in any of the existing pagan sanctuaries of the Greco-Roman worlds.

No stipulations whatever are made by *halakhah* for the general external appearance of the synagogue. Indeed, revelation at the burning bush, at Sinai, and in the Tabernacle surely teaches that no place is devoid of the

Divine Presence—neither the lowliest of trees, nor the barest of mountains, nor a wooden sanctuary. As has been seen, *halakhah* governs only very specific elements of synagogue design—chiefly orientation, location, height, lighting, and provision for separate seating for men and women. The last-mentioned need could be answered by the basilica plan, in which columns surrounded a central space, with a gallery on top of the interior porticoes. Beyond those elements, the only basic requirements of the interior are an ark in which to house the Torah scrolls, a *bimah* from which they are read, and—in Ashkenazi communities—a separate lectern or *ammud* for the prayer-leader. The arrangement of the essential elements of the interior has been dictated by the function of the synagogue as conceived in diverse communities and in various periods. The architectural plan of the building has in turn been dictated by this interior arrangement, as well as by the styles prevailing at a particular time and place, so that over the ages synagogues have been built in nearly every form and style conceivable.

Early Synagogues
Archaeological evidence of synagogues has been discovered in the two Herodian fortresses of Masada and Herodium. At Masada the synagogue passed through two stages, the first probably from the time of Herod, in

The synagogue of the fortress of Herodium (left), showing benches along the walls. Bar mitzvah of young Israelis in the synagogue of Masada (right).

the first century B.C.E., the second certainly from the time of Zealot occupation. In the earlier, the E-shaped arrangement of columns is reminiscent of the transverse row of the Galilean synagogues; in the later synagogue at Masada a corner of the building was separated by a wall from the rest, probably to serve as a receptacle for the Torah scrolls. In both stages of development there were stepped benches along three of the walls, leaving the wall opposite Jerusalem for the entrance. The Herodium synagogue is similar in plan, and likewise has a *mikveh* adjoining it.

In the Galilee, over fifteen synagogues have so far been identified, dating from the third and fourth centuries C.E. They are rectangular in plan, the largest (Capernaum) measuring 428 square yards, the smallest 131 square yards. The usual proportion of length to width is 11:10. They are built of stone ashlars and paved with stone. The gallery, which ran along three sides of the building (excluding the façade) rested on two rows of columns going lengthwise and one row across. A staircase giving access to the gallery was provided outside the building. Some of the synagogues had an annex, probably used for the storage of the (movable) Torah ark. Stone benches ran along two or three sides. In some synagogues

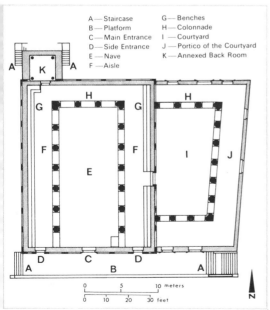

A — Staircase
B — Platform
C — Main Entrance
D — Side Entrance
E — Nave
F — Aisle
G — Benches
H — Colonnade
I — Courtyard
J — Portico of the Courtyard
K — Annexed Back Room

0   5   10 meters
0   10   20   30 feet

N

Plan of the Capernaum synagogue, c. third century C.E., and facade of the third century C.E. synagogue at Kefar Biram.

there was a porch outside the facade, in others a terrace accessible by staircase. In some cases a courtyard surrounded by porticoes was adjacent to the synagogue. This might have served as a place of rest during the services, or as a sleeping place for wayfarers.

With regard to orientation, the early type of synagogue presents a unique feature: the façades of these buildings are toward Jerusalem. It follows that if the worshipers entered through the main doors (usually three) in this facade, and if they had to face the Holy City in prayer, they had to make an about-turn after entering. In these synagogues no trace of a fixed place for the Torah ark has been found and it can be assumed that it was a movable object, carried or wheeled in for the services. The architectural origins of this type of synagogue, apart from its general basilica character common to the whole Greco-Roman world, are to be found in the Syro-Roman type of buildings. The architects of the synagogues were probably trained in the Syrian schools of architecture. From inscriptions we know the names of a few of them, in particular Yose the son of Levi "the craftsman" who built at Kefar Biram and Almah. In other cases it is not certain whether those who are mentioned as "making" (*abdun*) a synagogue were the builders or the donors. One feature is noticeable in synagogues of all types: no one seems to have been able to afford to donate the whole building. The various parts were offered by separate donors and the gift of each duly recorded on a column, lintel, or "chair of Moses."

The execution of the buildings was in the hands of local craftsmen, who introduced a strong oriental element into the classical orders (mainly Corinthian) of the columns ordered by the architect. The architectural ornament of the exterior facade of these buildings was rich and varied. The builders, it seems, were interested in proclaiming the importance of the building in the life of the community, not only by its lofty position but also by the splendor of its decoration. Thus not only were the door and window lintels decorated with molded profiles, but they were often surmounted by conches set in a gable to which a rich floral decoration was added. The facade of the two-storied buildings was surmounted with a gable of the type known as "Syrian." It consisted of a triangular pedi-

ment with its base cut into by an arch. It seems probable that the corners
of the building had decorations in the form of lions or eagles. Some of
the lintels are of special interest because they had in the center a relief of
a wreath held by two winged figures. Occasionally the consoles flanking
the doors were made in the form of palm trees.

In contrast with this rich, almost flamboyant, exterior, the interior of the
building was kept deliberately bare. It was lit by windows above the
doors, the one facing the source of all light, Jerusalem, being the largest.
The columns within the building were smooth and stood on high pedestals;
the double-corner columns at the meeting of the three rows had heart-
shaped bases in section. The capitals were of a simplified Corinthian order. The architects, it appears, were interested in avoiding within the
synagogue anything which could distract the worshipers while at prayer.
One exceptional feature in this respect was the richly decorated frieze.
Scholars are still discussing the exact position of this architectural feature; most are inclined to place it over the wall of the women's gallery.
The frieze usually consisted of a running garland of acanthus or vine
scrolls, with various images and symbols set within medallions. The
symbols include a number of Jewish religious objects, such as the *menorah,*
the *shofar, etrog,* and *lulav,* and the holy ark. Geometric figures such as
the hexagram (Shield of David) or the pentagram (Seal of Solomon), and
the fruits of the land, in particular the "seven species," were also commonly used. Sometimes the tolerant attitude of the communities went so
far as to include images derived from the world of Greek mythology. At

A lintel from the *bet midrash* at Dabbûra, Golan Heights, showing two eagles
holding a wreath, and bearing the name of the second-century sage, Eleazar
ha-Kappar.

Part of the frieze from the synagogue at Capernaum, showing a hexagram and a pomegranate motif.

Capernaum a griffin and a capricorn were included in the decorations, while the artists at Chorazin went still further and featured such pagan elements as Hercules with his club, a centaur, a Medusa, a human face, and a vintage scene. Occasionally, even the symbol of the Romans, the eagle, was represented on synagogue lintels. All these, however, were in relief; the only three-dimensional sculpture depicted lions, such as those found at Chorazin. It is clear that these symbols were used in a general and non-pagan sense.

In the second half of the third century C.E., architects attempted modifica- *The Transitional* tions of various kinds. Sometimes these were made in existing buildings; *Type* a typical case is the synagogue of Bet She'arim in which an extra structure was built against the central door, blocking it. The two side doors were left for the entrance, but a new focus of worship was evidently created in the direction of Jerusalem. Other synagogues show a number of architectural experiments. In one of the early-type synagogues, that of Arbel (Irbid), a niche was included in the wall facing the façade, presumably as a fixed receptacle for the scrolls of the Law. At Eshtemoa (el-Samuʿ) in Judea, the problem of the relation of façade versus entrance was solved by changing the traditional plan. One of the long walls of the rectangle faced Jerusalem, while the entrance was through doors made in the short wall. A niche in the wall facing Jerusalem served as a focal point of worship. The same arrangement was adopted in the earlier of the two superimposed synagogues at Caesarea.

76

Plan of the fourth century C.E. synagogue at Eshtemoa.

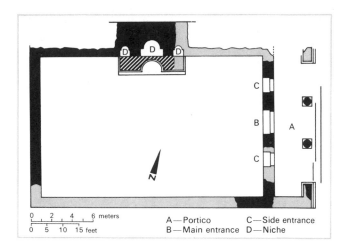

A—Portico   C—Side entrance
B—Main entrance   D—Niche

The transitional type also introduced another innovation in the architecture of the synagogues—mosaic pavements which now replaced the former stone slabs. These pavements were first decorated with geometric designs only, but from the fourth century onward (as we know from a saying of R. Abun recorded in the Jerusalem Talmud) figurative drawings were permitted. At Hammat one finds the earliest example of the standard type of synagogue pavement, figuring the signs of the Zodiac, with the sun in the center of the circle and the seasons in the four corners. The Zodiac circle was placed in the center of the pavement, with a representation of the ark flanked by two *menorot* beyond it. While the latter images are self-explanatory, it has been suggested that the Zodiac, representing the regular succession of months and seasons, also stood for the fixed holidays, and the succession of priestly *mishmarot* and *ma'amadot* in the Temple.

A new type may be said to emerge in the fifth century. This dating is confined by the fact that the synagogue of Gerasa was rebuilt as a church in 530 C.E. Once established, this type continued to be built until the eighth century. This later type was based on the pure basilica plan of the same kind as that used in contemporary churches. The building was elongated,

Fifth-Century Synagogues

77

with an apse pointing in the direction of Jerusalem. It sometimes had a court (atrium) and forecourt (narthex). The entrance was through three doors in the façade opposite Jerusalem and the interior was divided into a central nave and two aisles by two rows of columns. At the apse end a space was separated from the rest by a chancel screen, with columns and chancel slabs. Within, there was sometimes a lower space for the prayer leader. In the apse, which served as a receptacle for the Torah ark, there was another depression, used either as a place for keeping worn-out sacred texts or for the community chest.

The exterior of the building was kept plain and usually had a staircase leading to the women's gallery above the aisles. The lack of external ornament in these later-type synagogues is explained by the fact that they were erected under Byzantine rule, at a time when harsh anti-Jewish laws forbade the erection of new synagogues and only allowed old ones to be repaired when they threatened to collapse. The law was not strictly observed, but certain precautions had to be taken; hence the inconspic-uous outer aspect of the synagogues. Indeed, at Ḥammat Gader the synagogue was hidden inside a building complex, with indirect entrances from two sides. As far as can be judged, the splendor of the buildings was now concentrated in the interior. This is shown by the mosaic pavements and the elaborate marble capitals and chancel screens.

In the design of the mosaic pavements of three synagogues of this later type there is a combination of the Torah ark motif and the Zodiac, with biblical scenes: at Bet Alfa there is a representation of the Offering of Isaac; at Gerasa, Noah's Ark; and Daniel in the lions' den at Naaran. In these cases the Jews of that time do not seem to have had any qualms about treading on biblical imagery, including in one case (at Bet Alfa), a hand symbolizing God. At the same time they seem to have had much more respect for the written explanations added to the figures. At Naaran, for instance, when the images were removed as offensive, the writing accompanying each of them was carefully preserved. Other mosaics in synagogues follow the prevailing Byzantine trend toward a closely-knit design that divided the surface into a series of medallions. The basic ele-

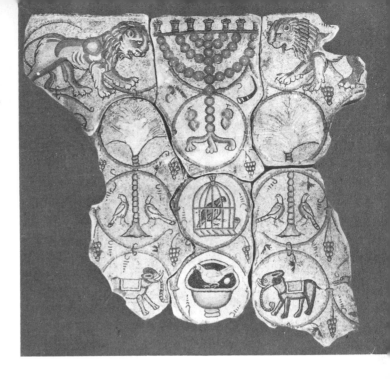

Detail of the mosaic floor of the synagogue of Maon, showing a *menorah, shofar, lulav,* and other traditional motifs.

ment is usually an amphora flanked by peacocks; a twisted wine trellis issued from the mouth of the jug and formed medallions with images of animals inside them. This decoration occurs at Maon and Gaza; both pavements are the product of the same Gaza factory. In the Gaza pavement (508/9 C.E.) the image of King David as Orpheus is added, while at Maon (c. 530) there are representations of animals to which a wedge-shaped part has been added, with specifically Jewish symbols, such as a *menorah* with lions guarding it, a palm tree, a *shofar,* an *etrog* and a *lulav.* In later synagogues (Ḥammat Gader, Jericho and En-Gedi), there seems to have been an increasing reluctance to use representations of living beings: at Ḥammat Gader there are only two lions, and in Jericho all images are absent; at En-Gedi the designs have been replaced by an inscription.

The only synagogues which carry actual dates are those of Gaza and Bet Alfa (518–27 C.E.). Of the artists, only the names of the makers of the Bet

Alfa pavement have been preserved: Marinos and his son Hannaniah. It is interesting to note that the same two artists worked on the pavement of a synagogue which was apparently Samaritan at Bet-Shean, not far from Bet Alfa. As could be assumed concerning the Samaritans, who were restricted in their biblical lore to the Written Law, the ornaments were much more austere than those in the Jewish synagogues: only the ark of the Law and flora or geometric ornaments were allowed. The same is true of the Samaritan synagogue at Shaalbim.

The finds of synagogues in the Diaspora cover a wide geographical and chronological range, from the Hellenistic to the Byzantine. Among the earliest is one at Delos, which must antedate 69 C.E., and one of the latest that of Aegina, sixth century C.E. On the whole the development of the Diaspora synagogues follows the same lines as those of Erez Israel. The second-century synagogue of Sardis (Asia Minor), recently excavated, is the largest and most sumptuous of those of the Diaspora, as befits the wealthy community it served. It is integrated within the central market-place of the town, together with a gymnasium and other public buildings, thus indicating the status of the Jews of Sardis. The synagogue consists of a courtyard and an elongated basilica, with an apse at its western end and the entrances at the east. Thus the elders sitting on semicircular benches within the apse faced Jerusalem, but the position of the rest of the congregation is in dispute. The synagogue had a reading table set in front of the apse and two raised platforms between the doors of the east side. The various ritual objects were beautifully worked.

Outside Erez Israel

Of the later synagogues, one of the best known is that of Dura Europos on the Euphrates. Two buildings were found there, one superimposed on the other; the later one is dated 244/5 C.E. They are similar in plan, with a broad central room and three entrances on the east side, a niche for the ark in the west (facing Jerusalem), and benches round the walls. The synagogue of Dura Europos was hidden between other houses and had an indirect entrance, which was even more obscure in the later building. This synagogue was decorated by famous frescoes. Of the synagogues of the fourth century in the Diaspora, three are outstanding: that of Ostia, in

The niche for the Torah scrolls in the synagogue of Dura Europos, dating from the middle of the third century C.E.

The mosaic floor of the synagogue of Hammam Lif in Tunisia, dating from the fourth century C.E.

which the original arrangements resemble those at Sardis, had a semicircular *bimah* facing Jerusalem. The entrances were later changed by the addition of an aedicula to house the ark. The synagogue of Naro (Hammam Lif in Africa) was biaxial, with the main entrance on the south, and a subsidiary entrance on the west. There was a small interior apse with seats, a special room for the "instruments," a *bimah,* and a room for women. The principal donor was a woman, Julia. This synagogue is distinguished by a richly decorated mosaic pavement with images of animals and plants.

From the Middle Ages to the Eighteenth Century

The relatively small number of Jews in any particular place, and the existence of rich building traditions among their neighbours, left little room for the development of a specific Jewish art of building. The synagogue alone developed into an architectural creation of Jewish origin, each region in each period finding its own architectural solutions to the halakhic and practical requirements that presented themselves.

Medieval Jewish communities were extremely small, and this determined *Formation* the intimate scale of synagogue buildings, which were sometimes hardly *of the Interior* more than mere rooms set aside for public prayer. Moreover, the insecurity of Jewish life, and the frequent threat and fear of the surrounding environment, were factors which determined building plans. In some places regulations by the Church authority or by the secular government often prohibited the building of new synagogues and sometimes even the enlargement of old buildings. Further, while Jewish Law decreed that synagogues had to be higher than the surrounding buildings, ecclesiastical regulations required that they be lower than Christian places of worship. Frequently, such laws were spitefully interpreted. It can therefore be assumed that the tradition that grew up of placing the level of the synagogue floor below that of the ground outside was not simply in accordance with Psalm 130:1 ("From the depths did I call Thee, O Lord"), but was also the result of the need to increase the height of the interior without transgressing the law restricting the external height. Until the 18th cen-

82

tury the Jews endeavoured to retain a degree of external unpretentiousness in their synagogue buildings, however splendid they were internally. This phenomenon is found throughout the lands of the Jewish Diaspora—and the few exceptions are generally the product of a temporary relaxation on the limitations.

The synagogue interior presents a peculiar architectural problem in terms of the interrelationship between the Torah ark, the *bimah,* and the congregation. In many of the Diaspora communities of long standing, the ark appears in the form of a small apse or a niche in the east wall oriented to Jerusalem. Although the ark housing the scrolls was one of the most salient features of the building, it did not as yet dominate the interior completely, for the synagogue was also a "house of assembly," a meeting place for the congregation. Had prayer been the synagogue's exclusive activity, it would have been natural for the ark attached to the wall which the congregation faced to become the architectural focus, imposing axial trends or a feeling of length. But in the synagogue interior there is another focal item, namely the *bimah*—the dais from which the service is conducted. The relative proximity between two foci in one interior, the ark situated in the east wall and the *bimah* at the center, and a search for a balance between them, constituted, and still constitutes, an aggravating architectural problem. The relationship between the two and their reciprocal relation to the entire interior space is the principal conceptual and ideological factor in synagogue design.

When Europe came to be dominated by the late Renaissance and Baroque styles, the ark attained an importance expressed by its size and by the high level of its artistic execution. It was in this period that monumental built-in arks were created, such as can be seen in Diaspora communities in modern times. Existing synagogues began to be rebuilt and fitted with arks in the new style. Generally, however, European Jewry was conservative in matters of form, still clinging to earlier cultural conceptions, and using medieval idioms, while Renaissance architecture was at its height.

The segregation of sexes during prayer, introduced in ancient times and necessitating a women's section, attached but separate, continued in the synagogues of the Middle Ages. In the early synagogues a gallery sometimes served this function. Often the place allotted to women was a separate hall on the same level as the main space. The most famous example of this is the synagogue at Worms. Sometimes the women's section was below the level of the main congregation hall or even actually beneath it as, for example, in Provencal synagogues. In the synagogue of Don Samuel ha-Levi Abulafia in Toledo (subsequently the Church of "El Transito"), built in the 14th century, there was an upper gallery alongside the rectangular hall. It was only at the end of the 16th century, when the presence of the woman in the synagogue became commonplace, that the women's section acquired full importance. Synagogues began to be built with well-planned women's accommodation, the first such being the major synagogues of Venice, the Veneto and other Italian communities, and the synagogue of Isaac Jacobowicz at Cracow, Poland. Generally in the medieval period the *ezrat nashim,* as the women's section was named, was added to the existing building as an external "lean-to." The gallery (or galleries) pitched internally over a row of columns is a later development, of which the earliest famous example is the Spanish-Portuguese synagogue of Amsterdam (1685).

The synagogues of medieval Central Europe fall into two main types: synagogues with a twin-naved hall, and those with a vaulted or timber-roofed single nave. When Jewry was forced to borrow a type of building suited to its needs, it borrowed not from the Church but from the existing secular forms. The choice was usually a building which was as far as possible removed from the monumental religious character of the Christian church. Jews took as their models town halls or monastic refectories,

The Worms synagogue, with the women's section at left. In the foreground is the *bimah.*

84

which were usually vaulted structures with either a single or double nave, the latter distinguished by a row of columns carrying the intermediate portion of the double span. When copying the ribbed ceilings prevalent at the time, a fifth rib was sometimes added. This helped perhaps to avoid the cruciform vaulting.

The oldest building surviving in its original form before it was destroyed *The* by the Nazis in November 1938 was the renowned synagogue of Worms. *Double-Naved* Its construction began in 1034, but the structure underwent a fundamental *Hall* change at the end of the 12th century, when buildings in the city were marked by a transition from the early to the late Romanesque style. The columns and their capitals and the portal whose details and decoration are identical with those of the columns (also the chandeliers, known from description only), may have been the work of a Jewish artist. An inscription preserved for nearly 800 years on one of the columns read:

> The pride of the two columns
> He wrought diligently,
> Also the scroll of the capital,
> And hung the lamps.

The two-naved hall is a centralizing space, the *bimah* being placed midway between the two columns. The women's section attached to the main building's north wall at the same level is hardly smaller, and was built in 1213.

The second well-known Central European synagogue of this style was the old synagogue in Prague, Altneuschul (literally "The Old-New Synagogue" or *Al tenai*, "on condition"). The very narrow windows shed a gloom on the interior in keeping with the traditional folk stories woven around this synagogue. The Altneuschul was built at the end of the 14th century and is unique in the Middle Ages for its impressive exterior—so different from the other synagogues of that period. This can be explained by the fact that the building was built in the heart of a large Jewish quarter and there was no fear of offending a hostile environment.

85

Another type of synagogue building in Central Europe in the Middle *The*
Ages was the vaulted single-cell hall, i.e., a structure consisting of one *Single-cell*
nave. There were, of course, timber-roofed synagogues without stone *hall*
vaults, often with open woodwork, in rare cases with wood panel ceilings. The best-known single-nave synagogue, without stone vault and
with visible roof trusses, was at Erfurt. Many were, however, proper
stone-vaulted Gothic single-cell buildings. Among the few that still exist,
or existed up to World War II, were Bamberg, Miltenberg, Leipnick, and
also the Pinkas-Shul built in the 13th century in Prague. The rest, which
developed particularly in Bohemia and Galicia, are known from records,
drawings, and documents. The longitudinal axis was later often enhanced
by the addition of the women's accommodation alongside the main
building. It usually had small windows the full length of the interior.
These late medieval rectangular synagogues were equipped with built-
in arks in a niche or small apse. The *bimah* retained its central position.

Most of the synagogues of Poland and Eastern Europe, including all the
wooden ones, were destroyed by the Nazis during World War II. A few
survived, and some of these have been restored.

Three Prague synagogues. Left to right: the single-vaulted Pinkas-Shul,
the Altneuschul, and the Renaissance Klauz Synagogue.

From the end of the 16th century the Jews of Poland developed a specific synagogue architecture. On the other hand, the Jewish communities of Bohemia and Galicia, which lived in comparative prosperity in Catholic lands, absorbed the Renaissance and Baroque architecture even in detail. The majestic Klauz Synagogue of Prague, built at the end of the 16th century and altered in the 17th, was barrcl-vaulted, and stuccoed with plant, scroll and flower ornamentation in the local Renaissance idiom. Cracow, likewise a city with a magnificent building tradition in the medieval and Renaissance styles, boasted barrel-vaulted synagogues with high lunettes; the western women's gallery was typically placed over the entrance lobby, and screened off from the main hall by elegant arcades on Tuscan columns. Cracow's oldest vaulted synagogue bears the name of one of that city's most brilliant sons, the halakhic authority Rabbi Moses Isserles.

At the beginning of the 19th century waves of migrants from Bohemia and Moravia carried the vogue of square vaulted synagogues to Germany, where ornamentation was added in the pronounced Baroque style current there.

The above-described building tradition of Bohemia and Moravia was a direct result of the work of non-Jewish architects or of close contacts with the respective environments of the various major cities. However, with the growing isolation of Jews from the European environment after the Middle Ages, Jewry created a world of its own, notably in the midst of Polish society. Within this world, there flowered an independent art. At first this was of a folk character, which expressed itself in decorative painting and in various arts and crafts, penetrating eventually into the building crafts.

The layout and space-form of the stone synagogues with four pillars ori- *The* ginated in Eastern Europe from this independent approach. Centralized *Four-Pillared* buildings for worship were always known in Europe and the Middle East. *Hall* Roman and Early Christian mausolea, Byzantine four-pillared churches on a square plan, Crusader temple-churches and baptisteries employing

87

the columned or pillared space-within-space layout, are an important species in architectural history. There were even Gothic four-pillared small churches and chapels. But none of those was so involved with the idea of a concentric plan. The principal problem was the *bimah* and the desire to emphasize its central position and overriding importance. Its expressive and forceful solution determined the connection of the building's shell with the *bimah* in a rigid manner, by including it in the internal space formed by the four pillars. This kind of space relationship was partly anticipated hundreds of years earlier by the double-naved two-pillared synagogue with the *bimah* between the columns. The two isolated cases with a single pillar (the Eger synagogue and the women's section at Worms) perhaps expressed an even stronger centralizing notion. It was of course possible to emphasize a centralized layout by other architectural means, as indeed shown in the domed synagogues throughout the centuries. But never was the centrally-designed *bimah* as strongly and meaningfully stressed as in this case when it was integrated in the structural system of pillars, vaulting and buttressing, creating a four-pillared sub-space within the shell of the building. Synagogues where the four pillars create a close group, include the buildings at Rzeszow (Reia), Maciejow, Vilna, Nowogrodek, Lutsk and Lancut.

A less absolute type-layout was also in use, in which the four supporting pillars which contained the *bimah* divided the hall into nine equal bays. The Vorstadt synagogue of Lvov and the synagogue at Zholkva are the most characteristic examples of this type of hall.

The four-pillared synagogue was a full answer to the problem of a centrally conceived liturgical function. As such it may be considered one of the highlights of synagogue architecture. Its validity may be seen in the fact that many of the contemporary and later wooden synagogues were designed with four timber posts surrounding a *bimah*. This was structurally superfluous as timber can bridge relatively large spans. It is also interesting to note the prevalence of similar concepts in the vernacular synagogue architecture of North Africa. The four-pillared, vaulted, 14th-century stone synagogue of Tomar, Portugal, is also relevant in this context. **88**

Sephardi Torah-scroll case, silver gilt on wood, Baghdad, 1852. The twin glass plates on the inside of the cupola are inscribed with biblical passages.

North African Torah-scroll ornaments, 19th century.
Mantle: velvet embroidered with silver and gold thread,
backed with leather, Morocco. *Rimmonim:* silver, partly
gilt, and enamel.

The four-pillared synagogue of Lancut, in a drawing by Zygmund Vogel,
late 18th century. At right, the synagogue of Gardaia, Algeria, with the *bimah*
also located between the central pillars.

Four-columned synagogues in Palestine include the Ashkenazi synagogue
of the Ari and the Sephardi synagogue of Rabbi Isaac Aboab at Safed,
the Avraham Avinu synagogue at Hebron, destroyed during the Arab
massacre of 1929, and the Prophet Elijah and the Istanbuli synagogues,
both in the Old City of Jerusalem, destroyed in 1948 and rebuilt in 1972.

The exterior appearance of European synagogue buildings often reflected *Synagogues*
local conditions. Thus many of them, especially those which stood outside *as Fortresses*
the city walls, were built as fortresses for the purpose of defence against
Cossacks or Tartars. They usually included a roof surrounded by a fortified parapet equipped with loopholes and sometimes with small towers,
as part of the arcaded attic-story typical of the Polish Renaissance. This
exterior characterized the Vorstadt synagogue of Lvov (the entrance
foyer of which featured a pillory), and the Zholkva, Pinsk and other 17th-
century synagogues. In Lutsk, in Volhynia, part of the fortress built by
Prince Witold was rebuilt as a fortified synagogue, with the permission of
King Sigismund III. From the gunmounts on the roofs, Jews served as
gunners whenever the city was under enemy attack, and underground tun-
nels led from the synagogue to other key buildings in the city. This synagogue withstood the fires and enemy attacks of centuries; in our generation, the authorities of the Ukrainian S.S.R. have converted it into a
movie theater.

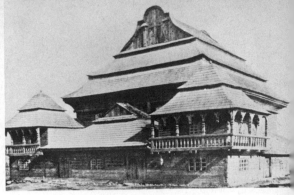

The fortress-synagogue of Zholkva, c. 1695. Watercolor by Nathan Pohlenberg, 1913. At right, the wooden synagogue of Wolpa, Poland, early 18th century.

The Polish wooden synagogues are a unique architectural phenomenon. *Wooden*
The wooden synagogue is the best known expression of a Jewish folk art *Synagogues*
which developed especially from the mid-17th century under the influence
of the Polish vernacular traditional building arts and spread over the
entire Jewish settlement area of Eastern Europe. Side by side with the
four-pillar stone synagogues the numerous wooden synagogues built in
the same period were a specific Jewish expression. Many conjectures exist
on their origin; the simplest is that they came quite naturally through
the tradition of carpentry preserved among the local population which
was in the habit of constructing many of its buildings in timber. Proofs
exist that many or perhaps most of these synagogues were designed and
built by Jewish craftsmen. The Jewish builder, aware of his special theme,
began by giving the eaves an upward curve, and piled roof upon roof. In
a later period the form of building becomes quiet and restrained, but in
the 17th century the synagogues were imaginative, dynamic compositions
inside and out, of a complex design. The plan was generally simple. The
measurements of the interior were normally about 15 square meters. The
women's hall was an annex, or sometimes built as an internal gallery.
Characteristic is the additional "winter room," designed as a shelter for
very cold weather, and generally plastered to facilitate heating.

These synagogues sometimes had a quiet and restrained exterior and contained wooden columns in the classical Tuscan order such as were com-

90

mon in the manor houses of landed gentry in the region. Inside was a very complex timber vaulting, adorned with paintings and wood carvings. A number of wooden synagogues were built in this style in Germany. The painted wood-panelling of one of the best-known ones, that of Horb, may be seen at the Israel Museum of Jerusalem.

From the point of view of language and art form the Spanish Jews were *Spain* part of the Islamic civilization, as is evidenced in their synagogue buildings. Those built during the Golden Age of Muslim Spain did not survive, but even those built in Christian Spain were of Moorish design. To adorn their synagogue walls the Jews employed verses from the Bible, written in elegant Spanish characters, in emulation of their Muslim neighbors, who adorned their mosques with verses from the Koran. The two best-known synagogue buildings in Spain are at Toledo. One seems to have been built in the second half of the 13th century by Joseph ibn Shushan. It was confiscated at the beginning of the 15th century by the Church authorities and was ultimately known as the Church of Santa Maria la Blanca. Like most medieval synagogues, this building is modest in its exterior and splendid within. Its plan and structure are characteristic of a mosque. Four long arcades, which carry a flat beam-ceiling, divide the interior into five bays. The arches are horseshoe-shaped and the pillar capitals are richly carved. The pillar bases in the two central colonnades are adorned with glazed tiles. Small circular windows in the western wall apparently belonged to the women's hall, which no longer exists. Despite the building's relatively small size the interior looks spacious, due to the rhythm created by the horseshoe arches and the columns.

The second building (which later became the El Transito Church) is in the former ancient Jewish quarter of Toledo. It was the synagogue of Samuel ha-Levi Abulafia, minister of Pedro the Cruel, and built about the year 1357. The plan is that of a rectangular hall of long proportions. The walls are decorated with carved *mudejar* foliage. Lines of verses from the Psalms alternating with decorative patterns surround the hall beneath, and above is the arcaded clerestory. The walls of the women's section are decorated with ornamental inscriptions of verses from the Song of Miriam. The niche

91

The former synagogue of Samuel ha-Levi Abulafia, showing an alabaster grill, and carved stucco decoration.

in the eastern wall was initially made for the ark, and inscriptions on each side of it record the erection of the building by Samuel Abulafia. The windows of the clerestory are fitted with alabaster grilles, admitting a diffused light.

Many synagogues in Oriental countries still exist. The great synagogue *Arab* of Baghdad was described by the traveler Benjamin of Tudela in the 12th *Countries* century as a building which apparently contained a columned hall opening onto a courtyard, as in a typical mosque, and magnificently adorned with ornamental lettering similar to that of Spanish synagogues. The famous synagogue at Fostat was a Coptic basilica built in the ninth century. The Aleppo synagogue resembled in principle the layout of the ancient mosques of Cairo—Amru and Ibn-Touloun—both of the internal courtyard type. It had its separate, roofed *bimah* in the middle of the courtyard, where normally the mosque well is placed. The congregation was here seated in the porticoes surrounding the courtyard, and the ark was placed analogically to the *mihrab*. This is the most pronounced case of Islamic influence on synagogue design.

Jews had lived in Italy from the beginning of the Christian Era and they *Italy* preserved ancient local traditions. Italy had also absorbed Ashkenazi Jews, and, after the expulsion of 1492, exiles from Spain. Jews from the

The courtyard of the Aleppo synagogue, with an outdoor *bimah*.

Levant also established merchant outposts, notably in Venice. The synagogues in Italy, as in the other Diaspora centers, generally lacked exterior distinction, nor was anything novel introduced in the way of structure. Very little is known about the seating layout and position of the *bimah* in early Italian synagogues: the characteristic bipolar hall took shape only in the sixteenth and seventeenth centuries. This was an interior plan whereby the ark and the *bimah* were placed at the opposing ends of an axial layout. The intimate spatial schemes which resulted, constitute the unique contribution of Italian Jewry to architecture.

In some of them highly imaginative variations occurred. In Pesaro and Ancona, the *tevah* which is attached to the western wall is built on columns one story high above hall floor level, permitting axial entry into the hall facing the ark.

One of the most beautiful examples was the Sephardi synagogue at Ferrara, built in the middle of the 17th century and later remodeled. Here the *bimah* was placed opposite the ark in a studied and disciplined spatial coordination. But in most cities, more especially in the north, a solution took shape which placed the *bimah* against the western wall and elevated it. Most important was the almost universally practiced seating layout, rather like that of the British House of Commons', the congrega-

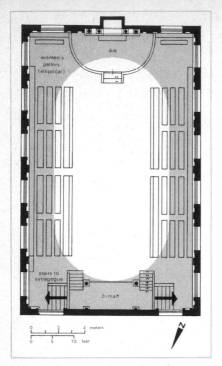

The bipolar plan of the Spanish synagogue, Venice (left), and the elevated *bimah* of the Spanish synagogue, Pesaro (right). Below: the relocated eighteenth-century synagogue of Conegliano Veneto.

94

tion being seated in two equal parts facing each other and divided by the aisle or "walk" connecting *bimah* and ark. Thus every worshiper could equally face both foci, and the ancient troublesome space conflict was at last resolved.

Apart from the bipolar spatial solution, the Italian synagogues left to Jewish art a fine tradition of skilled craftsmanship and furnishing. Torah-arks from Italy may be found in several international museums. Some of the small Italian communities, now finally dissolved, have recently transferred all their furnishings to Israel in order to be set up anew in synagogues there. The furniture of the synagogue of Conegliano Veneto has now been refitted at the Italian Synagogue in Jerusalem, while that of Vittorio Veneto has been fully reconstructed in the Israel Museum in Jerusalem.

The Nineteenth Century
With some exceptions, 19th century synagogue architecture was of a rather low general standard. The Jews in Western Europe and the U.S. gained emancipation and rose to prominence during this period, and erected large and ambitious buildings. There were as yet few Jewish architects, however, so that the architectural requirements of Jewish religious law were often interpreted somewhat insensitively by others. Since the 19th century lacked any single coherent architectural style of its own, the result could often be stylistic uncertainty, overloaded ornament unrelated to structure, and synagogues in Egyptian, Greek, Roman, Moorish, Romanesque, Gothic, Renaissance, Baroque, or other styles, or sometimes an unconvincing mixture of several of these. All this, however, was only apparent in the second half of the century. During the first half, synagogues generally possessed an appearance of dignity and restraint, and continued to be built in the classical tradition, but with a new emphasis on an archaeologically accurate revival of Greek and Roman architectural detail.

A very few synagogues, mostly in Central Europe and America, were affected by the mid-century Gothic revival, but the style was generally used only in details. It was felt to be too exclusively associated with Christianity, and the Jewish community adopted the Moorish style instead

95

The Plum Street Temple
in Cincinnati, Ohio, built
in 1866, showing strong
Moorish influence.

as that most suitable for the large city synagogue, perhaps partly owing
to its association with the golden age of Spanish Jewry. The style was carried by German congregations to the United States, where it was widely
adopted, as in Temple Emmanuel, New York (1868), Rodef Shalom,
Philadelphia (1869–70), and Plum Street Temple, Cincinnati, Ohio (1866),
with its 13 domes and two minarets.

The Early Twentieth Century

At the end of the 19th century architects began to react against the exuberant ornamentation of the preceding period. At first this reaction expressed itself in a simplification of design rather than in a complete abandonment of historical revivals, but later architects, influenced by func-
tionalist theories, produced stark synagogues without conscious reference
to any previous period. The abandonment of historical precedents made
it possible to some extent for architecture to reflect its contemporary

96

The Jeshurun Synagogue in Jerusalem, built in the mid-1930's.

historical and climatic environment. The modern synagogue in Erez Israel is a case in point. A synagogue at Ḥadera (1935) includes a watchtower and a courtyard to provide shelter for 2,000 people in case of attack. The Jeshurun synagogue, Jerusalem (1934–35), features small windows, and the synagogue at Herzliyya (1950) features large perforated sunscreens, to reduce the intake of the strong Mediterranean sunlight. A small intake of light is also a feature of the Hebrew University (1957) and the Hebrew Union College (1962) synagogues in Jerusalem.

The Contemporary Period

Contemporary synagogue architecture has rarely been successful in solving the problems raised by the need for reconciling the traditional values accumulated during the history of synagogue building, with modern social, economic, and architectural needs. One of the key issues in modern architecture has been the development of new forms to replace those abandoned in the process of evolution away from the styles of the past. The new technology and the stylistic freedom which prevail have opened up almost unlimited opportunities for the architect, with the result that the range of possibilities has, in a sense, impeded the formulation of fixed types of buildings for particular uses. In most cases, a combination of functional and aesthetic considerations has produced satis-

97

factory solutions, but the religious building, with its special requirements, has perhaps more than any other kind of structure posed serious difficulties for the architect in search of significant forms. During the nineteenth and early twentieth centuries, particularly in the U.S., architects drew upon such varied themes as the classical Greek temple, the Moorish mosque, the Gothic cathedral, the Byzantine Romanesque church, and the Colonial American Church. Temple Emmanuel in New York City, designed in 1930, has a combination of Romanesque portals, Gothic flying buttresses, and Moorish towers.

Since 1945 the contemporary synagogue has been not merely a house of worship, but in many instances a community center including a school, administration offices, gymnasium, and assembly hall. The best synagogue is often the most straightforward expression of its intended functions. Among the least successful designs are those which depend on symbolism in determining the plan of the structure. The value of the visual symbol is lost because the congregation is inside the space and unable to see the external form. It is in the field of ritual objects and the furnishings of the building, that symbolism finds its proper place.

In Europe After World War II
In the postwar period in Europe, few radical changes in planning were generally adopted, though from the late 1950s synagogues began to be constructed with main halls convertible for non-devotional purposes, and were built as part of a social complex including communal centers, old-age homes and other buildings, as in the United States. The visual effect was generally lighter than in the case of the solid and austere synagogues of the period between the wars. After World War II a number of synagogues were built by the small returning Jewish communities in Germany, where nearly all previous synagogues had been destroyed by the Nazis. In the case of the Community House in West Berlin (1959) fragments of the neo-Romanesque synagogue built on the site in 1912 and destroyed by the Nazis were preserved and placed in startling juxtaposition to the new building, as a reminder of the tragic fate of the German Jews.

The new Community House of West Berlin, built in 1959, showing fragments of the former Fasanenstrasse Synagogue incorporated into the façade.

9. THIS IS MY GOD AND I WILL GLORIFY HIM

Due to the partial prohibition of plastic arts, Jews found an outlet for their artistic abilities in the synagogue and in producing ceremonial objects. The high regard in which the fashioners of religious art were held is evident from the biblical description of Bezalel as being filled "with the spirit of God, in wisdom, and in understanding, and in knowledge, and in all manner of workmanship." The rabbis, commenting on the verse "This is my God and I will glorify Him," declare it meritorious to fulfill God's precepts with attractive objects such as "a beautiful *sukkah,* a beautiful *shofar,* beautiful fringes and a beautiful Torah scroll." In other words—the Jew should use aesthetically pleasing objects in the performance of his religious duties.

Symbolism
This obligation was well fulfilled in the synagogue. Synagogues from earliest times were decorated with murals and mosaic floors portraying Jewish history, ceremonial objects and various religious concepts. The artists— and the congregants who used the synagogue—were not averse to depicting even human beings. Many of the symbols were apparently borrowed from the non-Jewish environment and several even smack of pagan sym-

99

The naked figure of Libra in the mosaic floor at Ḥammat-Tiberias.

bolism. In the mosaic floor of the synagogue at Ḥammat-Tiberias naked human forms are depicted in the zodiac panel; and this, in a synagogue in use at the same time that Tiberias was the seat of the Sanhedrin. In the center of that zodiac Helios is depicted driving a chariot.

This type of decoration seems to become more rare as the Middle Ages progress, but a great deal of artistic energy was invested in the various articles of furniture in the synagogue and in the ceremonial objects.

A common feature in the modern synagogue is stained-glass windows. Some are simply designs in colored glass aimed at creating desired lighting effects in the sanctuary, but most are designed on Jewish themes such as the festivals, ritual objects or specific events in Jewish history. Often they display a great deal of biblical and talmudic erudition and even incor-

Stained-glass windows flanked by ornamental Tablets of the Law at Temple Beth Zion, Buffalo, N.Y., designed by Ben Shahn, 1966.

100

porate apposite quotations. Perhaps the best known windows are the twelve made for the Hadassah Hospital in Jerusalem by Marc Chagall, which are a work of art in their own right. They represent the twelve tribes of Israel, and are replete with biblical and rabbinic allusions.

The Torah Scroll

The Torah scroll is the holiest and most important object in the synagogue. It is housed in the ark and it is taken out for public reading four times a week: during the morning services on the Sabbath, Mondays and Thursdays and in the Sabbath afternoon service, besides on festivals and fast days. It is also taken out for ceremonial circuits on Simḥat Torah. The scroll itself is handwritten on parchment and must be very exact in its wording; the slightest mistake can make it unfit for public reading.

Because of its importance the Torah scroll is "dressed" in various "garments" according to the different rites. Covering the scrolls in an Ashkenazi synagogue is a mantle through the top of which protrude the two staves, called *aẓei ḥayyim* ("trees of life"), on which the scroll is rolled. Mounted on these staves are two finials called in Hebrew *rimmonim* which may have developed from decorated knobs at the top of the antique *aẓei ḥayyim,* and an open crown (*atarah* or *keter*) sometimes surrounds both finials on top of the scrolls. In some communities the custom was to have a closed crown with no finials. The earliest mention of a crown appears in the year 1,000, in the responsum of a Spanish rabbi in answer to a question about the use of women's jewelry in its manufacture. Another early reference is in the records of the province of Arles, France, where a contract dated 1439 is recorded in which the Jewish community ordered a crown from a Christian goldsmith and also provided for the further embellishment of one they had. The Sephardi and Oriental Torah case is made of wood and is decorated in leather or metal. The two halves of the arch-shaped box are hinged and are opened like a book to reveal the Torah, which is read without being removed. The scroll is opened at the required column by manipulation of the staves which protrude from the top of the box and are surmounted by *rimmonim*.

The Garments

101

On the Ashkenazi Torah, over the front of the decorative mantle, a "breast-plate" or shield is suspended, on which the name of a festival is inscribed. The breastplate originated as a tab hung from the staves to designate the scrolls to be read on various occasions, such as the festivals or special Sabbaths, when more than one scroll is read. It is called a breastplate to recall that worn by the high priest in the Temple. The most common ones are heavily engraved with traditional symbols. Modern pieces tend to be simple and recall the design of the ancient priestly ornaments or consist simply of a lion of Judah or a tree of life, symbolising the Torah. *The Breastplate*

During the reading of the Torah it is forbidden to touch the parchment. A pointer or *yad* ("hand") is therefore used. The *yad* is frequently quite literally a hand with a pointing finger and is sometimes even encrusted with semiprecious stones, bracelets, and rings. The modern pointer is simply that—a pointer. *The Yad*

Reading a Sephardi Torah scroll made in Persia, 1799 (left). A silver Torah pointer combined with a *havdalah* spice-box, Prague, c. 18th century (right).

After the reading, the Torah scroll is rolled together on its *azei hayyim* and tied around by a wrapper which is usually a simple, long, wide ribbon. However, in some East European communities, the wrapper was made of a baby boy's swaddling cloth. The cloth was cut into strips, which were joined to form a long runner. This was embroidered or stencilpainted with the child's name, the traditional blessing that he grow up to Torah ("learning"), *huppah* ("marriage"), and *ma'asim tovim* ("good deeds"), and with pictorial representations pertinent to these subjects. Colorful pictures of animals or birds, reminiscent of the baby's name, were sometimes inserted in the remaining space. The little boy (at the age of four or five) brought this wrapper with him when he first visited the synagogue, and at his bar mitzvah the Torah read from was bound in his wrapper.

The Ark

In early synagogues the Torah scrolls were kept in a movable receptacle which was stored in a safe place when not in use. In the Dura Europos synagogue (c. 245 C.E.), a niche in the wall facing Jerusalem was fitted to receive the scrolls which were evidently placed in a low wooden cabinet. In ancient paintings and graffiti the scrolls are seen lying on shelves in open cabinets. During the Middle Ages the ark took the form of a tall, freestanding cupboard in which the scrolls were stored in an upright position. This form provided ample scope for decorative art and the ark, which is known among Ashkenazi Jews as the *aron ha-kodesh* and among Sephardim as the *heikhal,* was elaborately decorated with carved panels and even paintings. An additional feature was the twin tablets representing the Ten Commandments set on top of the structure. The tablets are often supported by animal figures, usually an upstanding lion on each side.

Wrappers with Torah, *huppah,* and floral motifs: Italy, 1602; Germany, 1737.

Baroque ark of the law at
Wlodawa, Poland, with
musical instruments (Psalms
137) and animals (Avot
5:20).

In the eighteenth century in Germany a baroque structure adorned with
columns, pilasters, broken cornices, pediments and vases became standard
and quickly spread to Eastern Europe where it was further adorned
with animal figures and openwork scrolls. Arks were often in the Oriental
style and featured bulbous domes and horseshoe arches. After World
War II the creation of the ark became an art form and many artists ex-
perimented with new and daring forms and materials.

Concealing the doors of the ark there is often, in the Ashkenazi rite, a *The*
hanging curtain called the *parokhet*. Not only are these frequently made *Parokhet*
of rich material, but there are often different sets for weekdays, Sabbaths,
festivals, and the High Holidays. Besides the personal inscription of the
donors, there are frequent motifs of floral arrangements, fountains, fruits,
grapevines, doves, eagles, and lions, as well as representations of all the
traditional implements of the Temple, especially fluted, twisted columns,

104

Torah crown, repoussé and perforated silver gilt, originally studded with
precious stones, Germany, 1793. The hands are raised in the priestly blessing.

Italian Torah ornaments. Mantle: silk embroidered with gold thread, 17th century. *Rimmonim:* silver, Padua, 18th century. Crown: silver, partly gilt, 1742. Breastplate: silver, 1776. In the background is a *parokhet* of embroidered Italian silk, Turkey, 18th century.

Bronze ark designed
by Luise Kaish
for Temple B'rith
Kodesh, Rochester,
N.Y., 1964.

reminiscent of the pillars which stood at the entrance to Solomon's
Temple. A popular decoration is a crown (symbolic of *keter Torah*—the
Crown of the Torah) supported by two lions. Frequently an upper
valance called the *kapporet* matches the *parokhet*. In Eastern Europe
in the Baroque period, the *parokhet* was sewn by ladies of the community,
often from bits of clothing worn on important occasions, a custom which
now seems to be returning in some American communities.

In front of the ark there is usually a light which is kept burning continu-
ously and which is hence known as the *ner tamid.* This light is a symbolic
reminder of the candelabrum (*menorah*) of the Temple and was originally
placed in a niche in the western wall of the synagogue in remembrance of
the position of the *menorah* in the Temple. In the course of time it was
moved to its present position, being generally suspended from the ceiling,
and adds to making the ark the focus of the congregants' attention.
Though originally an oil lamp, nowadays electricity is used. Sometimes

The
Ner Tamid

105

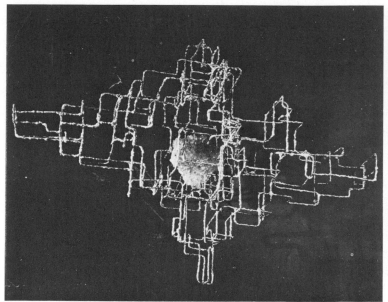

Contemporary *ner tamid* (left) designed by Ibram Lassaw for Temple Beth-El,
Springfield, Mass., and a 19th-century one from Casablanca.

the *ner tamid* is artistically fashioned of metal, with rays of light from
spot lamps reflecting from it. Like the other artifacts in the synagogue
the *ner tamid* too has served as a vehicle for artistic expression, each age
and location producing its characteristic forms.

Donating the light and its oil is considered a meritorious deed, and the
donors are specially blessed in the *mi she-berakh* prayer recited in the
synagogue every Sabbath.

In many synagogues, both ancient and modern, there is a cande- *Candelabra*
labrum, symbolic of that which stood in the Temple. It is, however, never
made to the specifications in the Bible but is only an approximate imitation since the *halakhah* forbids making an exact copy. Commonly the
synagogue also contains a Ḥanukkah candelabrum for use in the synagogue on that festival. **106**

The Bimah

One of the most important components of the synagogue service is the public reading of the Torah and it is natural that arrangements should be made to enable all the congregants to hear it as clearly as possible. This is achieved by conducting the reading from a raised platform known variously as the *bimah* (Hebrew for "platform"), *almemar* (Arabic, *al minbar* for "platform") or, exclusively among Sephardi Jews, *tevah* (Hebrew for "box").

The reading desk is covered by an embroidered cloth *(mappah)*. At the far edge of the desk there is sometimes a decorated horizontal rod, on which the upper part of the staves is rested in order to raise the scroll and put it on a slope. On the side, at times on the railing surrounding the *bimah*, are two protruding staves to hold the finials while the Torah is being read. *Halakhah* requires that the *bimah* be surrounded by a railing or parapet for safety reasons, and one authority prescribed that there be three steps leading to it.

Chizuk Amuno Synagogue, Baltimore, showing *bimah* and pulpits at front.

Examples of the *bimah* surviving from early times are simple in form and built close to the floor. In medieval Spain the *bimah* was a wooden platform raised high on columns, sometimes surmounted by a canopy and reached by a stairway. Until the Renaissance the *bimah* had a more dominant position than the ark; in Italy from the sixteenth century they were given equal emphasis by being located at opposite sides of the synagogue. In the synagogue at Worms (1175) the *bimah* was placed on the central axis between the two main columns and this became the usual arrangement among Ashkenazi Jews in Central and Eastern Europe. Later, the four central pillars which supported the vaulted ceiling of the synagogue were used as the framework of the *bimah* which thus became a roofed structure. The *bimah* has assumed curved, circular, octagonal and other forms, and all kinds of materials have been used for its construction.

Usually the *bimah* is located in the center of the synagogue with some rows *Position* of seating between it and the ark; in the Middle Ages, in some Sephardi synagogues, it was located at the rear of the synagogue.

In the nineteenth century a trend started in Reform synagogues to move the *bimah* from the center of the synagogue to the front, resulting in a stage on which the ark stood. This innovation was made in order to utilize the

The Tifereth Israel Synagogue, Caracas, showing central *bimah* and women's gallery.

108

seating space more effectively, but the end result was that the synagogue came to resemble a church more closely. The leading Orthodox rabbis of the time vehemently opposed the move and a proclamation was signed by 100 rabbis prohibiting worship in a synagogue of the new type. However, almost all Reform and Conservative and a number of modern-Orthodox synagogues have combined the *bimah* with the ark.

The Ammud

In most Ashkenazi synagogues the *bimah* is used only for the Torah reading and, where there is no pulpit, occasionally for the sermon; the *ḥazzan* leads the service from a special lectern (known as the *ammud*) in front and to the right of the ark. In some old synagogues this lectern was lower than the level of the rest of the synagogue, symbolic of the Psalmist's cry: "From the depths did I call Thee, O Lord." The lectern is also a vehicle for synagogue art, being richly decorated and ornamented, often with kabbalistic designs incorporating various scriptural quotations, and nearly always with the verse "I have set God before me always," and the aphorism "Know before whom you stand." This is to remind the *ḥazzan* of the seriousness of his task. In Sephardi and Oriental synagogues, however, the whole service is conducted from the *bimah,* and today certain Ashkenazi synagogues have likewise eliminated the *ammud.*

An elevated *bimah* (left) shown in a 14th-century Spanish *haggadah,* and an 18th-century octagonal *bimah* from Harburg, Germany (right).

Aleinu, prayer recited at the conclusion of every service; it is also the central theme of the additional service of Yom Kippur.

Almemar, see *Bimah.*

Amidah, main prayer recited at all services; also known as *Shemoneh esreh.*

Ammud, lit., pillar; reader's lectern in Ashkenazi synagogues.

Aron (ha-)kodesh, holy ark; receptacle in which the Torah scrolls are stored in the synagogue. Sephardi usage is *heikhal.*

Ashkenazi (pl. Ashkenazim), German or West-, Central-, or East-European Jew(s), as contrasted with Sephardi.

Bar mitzvah, ceremony marking the religious initiation of a boy at the age of 13.

Bat mitzvah, as above, for a girl at age 12.

Bet din, rabbinic court of law.

Bet knesset, synagogue.

Bet (ha-) midrash, school for rabbinic learning; often attached to, or serving as, a synagogue.

Bimah, platform from which the Torah is publicly read in the synagogue. Also called *almemar; tevah* in Sephardi usage.

Darshan, preacher.

Dayyan, member of rabbinic court.

Etrog, citron; one of the "four species" used on Sukkot.

Ezrat nashim, women's section in Temple and thus also in synagogue; in Yiddish known as *weibershul.*

Gabbai (pl. *gabbaim*), elected synagogue official.

Geonim, heads of the academies in post-talmudic period, especially in Babylonia.

Ḥabad, ḥasidic movement founded in White Russia.

Halakhah, rabbinic law.

Ḥanukkah, Feast of Lights, eight day festival beginning 25th Kislev (Dec.–Jan.) commemorating Hasmonean victory.

Ḥasid (pl. Ḥasidim), adherents of religious movement (Ḥasidims) founded in first half of the 18th century.

Havdalah, ceremony marking end of the Sabbath.

Hazzan (pl. *ḥazzanim*), precentor who leads the prayers in the synagogue. Also called *sheliaḥ ẓibbur.*

Heikhal, see *Aron (ha-)kodesh.*

Hekdesh, term used for hospice attached to synagogue.

110

Ḥerem, excommunication.

Ḥevrah, lit., society; voluntary association, usually for mutual aid.

Ḥuppah, nuptial canopy.

Kashrut, Jewish dietary laws.

Kehillah (pl. *kehillot*), community.

Kiddush, prayer of sanctification on the Sabbath and festivals; recited over wine or bread.

Kloyz, institution in Central and Eastern Europe for the study of rabbinics; usually also served as a synagogue.

Kohen (pl. *kohanim*), Jew of priestly (Aaronide) descent.

Kol Nidrei, prayer ushering in Yom Kippur.

Landsmannschaft, association on the basis of common place of origin.

Lulav, palm branch; one of the "four species" used on Sukkot.

Maggid (pl. *maggidim*), preacher; often itinerant.

Maẓẓah (pl. *maẓẓot*), unleavened bread eaten on Passover.

Meḥiẓah, partition separating men from women in synagogue.

Midrash, collection of rabbinic interpretations of, and homilies on, the Bible.

Mikveh (pl. *mikva'ot*), ritual bath.

Minyan (pl. *minyanim*), quorum of ten adult male Jews, the minimum required for communal prayer.

Mi she-berakh, prayer recited in synagogue.

Mishnah, earliest codification of Jewish oral law; completed in 3rd century C.E.

Mizraḥ, lit., east; synagogue wall at which the ark stands.

Ne'ilah, closing service of Yom Kippur.

Parnas, chief synagogue functionary.

Parokhet, curtain on the *aron kodesh*.

Passover, Pesaḥ, festival commemorating exodus from Egypt; begins on 15th of Nisan (Mar.–Apr.) and no bread is eaten for its duration (7 days; 8 in Diaspora), only *maẓẓah*.

Piyyutim, Hebrew liturgical poems.

Pletten, vouchers given to the needy entitling them to eat at congregants' homes.

Purim, festival commemorating delivery of Jews in Persia; celebrated on 14th (Jerusalem and a few other cities on 15th) of Adar (Feb.–Mar.).

Rav, rabbi.

Rebbe, ḥasidic rabbi.

Rosh ha-Shanah, 1st of Tishrei (Sept.–Oct.); Jewish New Year's festival observed for 2 days.

111

Sanhedrin, Jewish high court in Temple times.

Sefer Torah, Torah scroll.

Sephardi (pl. Sephardim), Spanish and Portuguese Jews and their descendants wherever resident; loosely used for Jews from Oriental countries. Contrasted with Ashkenazi.

Se'udah shlishit, third meal eaten on the Sabbath.

Shabbat ha-Gadol, the Sabbath preceding Passover.

Shabbat Shuvah, the Sabbath preceding Yom Kippur.

Shammash, beadle.

Shavu'ot, Pentecost, festival celebrated on 6th (and 7th in Diaspora) of Sivan (May–June).

Sheliah Zibbur, see *Hazzan*.

Shema, "Hear, O Israel" (Deut. 6:4), Judaism's confession of faith.

Shemoneh esreh, see *Amidah*.

Shofar, ram's horn, sounded on Rosh ha-Shanah and on other occasions.

Shtetl, Jewish small-town community in Eastern Europe.

Shtibl, hasidic prayer room.

Shul, synagogue.

Shulhan Arukh, authoritative code of Jewish law; compiled in 16th century.

Siddur, prayer book.

Sukkah, booth erected for use on Sukkot.

Sukkot, Tabernacles, festival beginning on 15th of Tishrei (Sept.–Oct.).

Takkanah (pl. *takkanot*), regulations supplementing the law.

Talmud, compendium of commentary on the Mishnah; completed in the 6th century C.E.

Tashlikh, ceremony of expiation performed on Rosh ha-Shanah near a body of water.

Tefillin, phylacteries, worn by male Jews during weekday morning service.

Tevah, see *Bimah*.

Tishah be-Av, 9th of Av (Jul.–Aug.); day of mourning for destruction of the Temples.

Weibershul, see *Ezrat nashim*.

Yeshivah (pl. *yeshivot*), academy devoted mainly to the study of Talmud and rabbinics.

Yom Kippur, Day of Atonement, 10th of Tishrei (Sept.–Oct.); most solemn day of the Jewish religious calendar.

Zoggeren, woman who led the prayer service for women in *ezrat nashim*.

ABBREVIATIONS TO SOURCES

Bible

Gen.	—	Genesis	Is.	—	Isaiah	Prov.	—	Proverbs
Ex.	—	Exodus	Ezek.	—	Ezekiel	Dan.	—	Daniel
Deut.	—	Deuteronomy	Hos.	—	Hosea	Macc.	—	Maccabees
Sam.	—	Samuel	Ps.	—	Psalms			

Talmud[1]

TJ   —   Jerusalem Talmud[2]

Tosef.	—	Tosefta	Meg.	—	*Megillah*	Sof.	—	*Soferim*
Ber.	—	*Berakhot*	Pes.	—	*Pesaḥim*	Sot.	—	*Sotah*
Ket.	—	*Ketubbot*	Sanh.	—	*Sanhedrin*	Suk.	—	*Sukkah*
Mak.	—	*Makkot*	Shab.	—	*Shabbat*	Taan.	—	*Ta'anit*

Later Authorities

Yad	—	Maimonides, *Yad ha-Ḥazakah*
Sh.Ar.	—	Shulḥan Arukh
EH	—	Even ha-Ezer
ḤM	—	Ḥoshen Mishpat
OḤ	—	Oraḥ Ḥayyim
YD	—	Yoreh De'ah

[1] References to the Mishnah are in the form: Meg. 1:3 (i.e., Tractate *Megillah*, chapter 1, mishnah 3); references to the Gemara are in the form: Meg. 17b (i.e. Tractate *Megillah*, page 17, second side). Thus a reference such as Suk. 4:1, 51b, refers first to the Mishnah and then to the Gemara.

[2] Otherwise all Talmud references are to the Babylonian Talmud.

SOURCES

page

1 Thus saith the Lord ... — Ezek. 11:16

1 The Talmud applies ... — Meg. 29a

1 More specifically ... — Meg. 29a

1 repeated mention ... Ezekiel — Ezek. 8:6, 14:1, 20:1

1 Talmud ascribes — Ber. 33a

2 to Moses ... Midrash ... —Targum Pseudo-Jonathan to Ex. 18:20; Midrash Yal., Ex. 408; Josephus, *Apion,* 2:175

2 Books of Maccabees ... —I. Macc. 3:48, 4:24

2 Daniel turned ... — Dan. 6:11; Ber. 31a

2 Solomon had said ... — I. Kings 8:38

2 So, too, the Temple's ... — Is. 56:7

4 Talmud ... Alexandrine — Suk. 51b; TJ, Suk. 5:1; Tosef. Suk. 4:6

4 Jerusalem had ... —Meg. 26a/b; TJ, Meg. 3:1; Tosef. Meg. 3(2):6; Sof. 11:3

4 number ... in Jerusalem ... —Ket. 105a

4 Temple Mount ... — Sot. 7:7–8; Yoma 7:1

5 Joshua ben Ḥananiah — Suk. 53a

5 Joshua ben Levi — Meg. 27a

5 Likewise, funds donated ... — Sh.Ar., YD 259:2

5 Noting the respective ... — Ber. 64a; Deut. Rabba 7:1

6 A town which among ... — Meg. 1:3, 17b; Sanh. 1:6

6 Maimonides ... — Yad. Megillah 1:8

6 *Kiddush* in the synagogue ... — Pes. 101a

7 eating and drinking in it — Meg. 28a

7 "for the reading of the Torah" — Sukenik, "Ancient Synagogues ..." p. 70

7 According to a description ... — Tamid 5:1

8 Hosea — Hos. 14:3

8 "*avodah* of the heart" — Sifre Deut. 41

9 "In the times to come ..." — Meg. 29a

9 One sage ... — Ber. 6a

9 "the whole world ..." — Is. 6:3

9 "... our dwelling place" — Ps. 90:1

9 "A man's prayer ..." — Ber. 6a

9 "one who has a synagogue ..." — Ber. 8a

9   'a bad neighbor' — cf. Jer. 12:14
9   "when a person . . ." — Ber. 6a
9   longevity — Ber. 7a
10 simultaneously — Ber. 8a
14 According to a *takkanah* . . . — Finkelstein, *Jewish Self-Government* . . .
     pp. 33, 48, 88, 335
15 Realizing that power . . . — Yoma 22b
15 The Midrash . . . — Leviticus Rabbah 25:1
17 The *hazzan* was required . . . — Sh.Ar., OH 53:4ff.
27 In the multitude . . . — Prov. 14:28 (cf. Midrash Prov. 28, 38a)
32 polemics — *Nogah ha-Zedek* ("The Splendor of Justice," 1818) states
     the Reformers' arguments: the Orthodox reply is given in *Elleh*
     Divrei ha-Berit ("These are the Words of the Covenant," 1819).
43 Those who mourn . . . — Is. 66:10 (cf. Taan. 30b)
43 Book of Micah — Mic. 3:12
43 Book of Zechariah — Zech. 8:4
43 From the Talmud — cf. Mak. 24b
54 Mordecai Kaplan — Mordecai M. Kaplan, "The Way I Have Come" in
     Mordecai M. Kaplan: An Evaluation (1952), p. 311
60 To exalt the house . . . — Ezra 9:9
60 Josephus — Antiquities, 14:258
60 The law . . . — Sh.Ar., OH 150:2
60 Indeed, the talmudic . . . — Shab. 11a
61 acceptable — Sh.Ar., OH 150:2, *Ba'er Heitev* ad loc, Mishnah Berurah, 8
61 Solomon — I Kings 8:30
61 Daniel — Dan. 6:11
62 Interestingly . . . — Tosef. Meg. 4:22
62 it is required — Ber. 8a
62 The Talmud warns — Ber. 34b
62 *Halakhah* . . . — Sh.Ar., OH 90:4
62 If a wall . . . — Sh.Ar., OH 150:4
63 In its description . . . — Suk. 5:2, 51b; Tosef. Suk. 4:1
63 Further sources . . . — Pirkei de-Rabbi Eliezer 23, 41
63 Following the Crossing — Ex. 15:20–21
64 References to . . . — Mordecai to Shab. Chap. 3., no. 311; *Sefer Maharil*
     (ed. Cremona, 1565), 38a, 50b, 59b   **115**

page

64 The abolition of the *mehizah* ... — *Hatam Sofer*, ḤM 190, OḤ 28; *Maharam Schick*, OḤ 77; *Teshuvot Beit Hillel*, 5; *Divrei Ḥayyim*, 18; *Zichron Shelomo*, 70–72

65 granted relief ... — Court Order of Sept. 21, 1959, Mount Clemens, Michigan; Superior Court of Pennsylvania, no. 178, Oct. term, 1954.

66 Behold they had done — Ex. 39:43

66 Accordingly the Shulḥan Arukh — Sh.Ar., OḤ 151

66 A multitude of responsa — e.g., Maharam of Rothenberg (ed. Prague), no. 439

66 One rabbi ruled ... — B. Levin, *Shemen Sason* (1904), 53 no. 27

67 The Shulḥan Arukh specifies ... —Sh.Ar., OḤ 154:3

69 If a congregation decides ... — Sh.Ar., OḤ 154, *Mishnah Berurah* 59

69 Since wedding ... — Gen. 22:17; Isserles to Sh.Ar., EH 61:1

99 This is my God ... — Ex. 15:2

99 Bezalel ... — Ex. 31:3

99 The rabbis ... — Shab. 133b

102 During the reading ... — Shab. 14a

109 The leading Orthodox rabbis ... — *Ḥatam Sofer*, OḤ 28; *Noda bi-Yehudah, Mahadura Tinyana*, OḤ 18; *Sedei Ḥemed, Asefat Dinim, Bet ha-Kneset*, 13

109 "I have set God ..." — Ps. 16:8

116

BIBLIOGRAPHY

Encyclopaedia Judaica, Jerusalem, 1971, under:
Synagogue, *Bet Midrash*, Rabbi, Preaching, *Ḥazzan*.

Abrahams, Israel, *Jewish Life in the Middle Ages*, London, 1869, 1932.

Baron, Salo W., *The Jewish Community*, Philadelphia, 1942.

Berman, Morton M., *The Role of the Rabbi, What Was, What Is, and What Shall the Rabbi Be*, New York, 1941.

Conquest, Robert (ed.), *Religion in the USSR*, London, 1968.

Edidin, Ben W., *Jewish Community Life in America*, New York, 1947.

Finkelstein, Louis, *Jewish Self-Government in the Middle Ages*, New York, 1964.

Freehof, Solomon B., *Reform Jewish Practice and Its Rabbinic Background*, Cincinnati, 1963.

Goodenough, Erwin R., *Jewish Symbols in the Graeco-Roman Period*, New York, 1953–68.

Gutmann, Joseph, *Jewish Ceremonial Art*, New York, 1964.

Hyamson, Albert M., *The Sephardim of England*, London, 1951.

Kampf, Avram, *Contemporary Synagogue Art*, Philadelphia, 1966.

Levitats, Isaac, *The Jewish Community in Russia*, New York, 1943.

Litvin, B., *The Sanctity of the Synagogue*, New York, 1959.

Levy, Isaac, *The Synagogue: Its History and Function*, London, 1963.

Loukomski, George K., *Jewish Art in European Synagogues*, London, 1947.

Mayer, Leo A., *Bibliography of Jewish Art*, Jerusalem, 1967.

Meier, Richard (ed.), *Recent American Synagogue Architecture*, N.Y., 1963.

Piechotka, Maria and Kazimierz, *Wooden Synagogues*, Warsaw, 1959.

Rostovtzeff, Mikhail I., *Dura-Europos and its Art*, Oxford, 1938.

Roth, Cecil, *The World of the Sephardim*, Tel Aviv, 1954.

Seiferth, Wolfgang S., *Synagogue and Church in the Middle Ages*, New York, 1970.

Sukenik, Elazar L., *Ancient Synagogues in Palestine and in Greece*, London, 1934.

Thiry, Paul *et al.*, *Churches and Temples*, New York, 1953.

Wischnitzer, Rachel, *The Architecture of the European Synagogue*, Philadelphia, 1964.

—, *Synagogue Architecture in the United States*, Philadelphia, 1955.

ILLUSTRATION CREDITS

Jerusalem, Department of Antiquities and Museums, p.4.
Jerusalem, C.A.H.J.P., p. 6, 13.
B. Picart, *Cérémonies et coutumes religieuses de tous les peuples du monde,* Amsterdam, 1723, p. 8.
Munich, Bayerisches Landesamt fuer Denkmalpflege, p. 11, 109.
Jerusalem, Israel Museum, p. 11, 16, 26, 79, 102, 103.
Photo David Harris, Jerusalem, p. 11, 16, 79, 94, 103, 106.
London Museum, p. 11.
J. Bodenschatz, *Kirchliche Verfassung . . .* 1748, p. 12.
Cecil Roth Collection, p. 16, 21, 24, 81, 86.
Courtesy *Black Star,* New York, Photo Jim Brown, p. 20.
London, Alfred Rubens Collection, p. 21.
Minhagim Book, Amsterdam, 1662, p. 23.
Photo R. Milon, Jerusalem, p. 26.
Shmuel Gorr Photo Collection, p. 27.
Jerusalem, Israel Museum Photo Archives, p. 29, 86, 93, 94.
Jerusalem, Yad Vashem Photo Archives, p. 30, 47, 104.
Bielefeld Municipality, p. 32.
Israel Government Press Office, p. 34, 35, 70, 72, 97, 100.
Courtesy E. Elias, Cochin, p. 36.
Israel Defence Forces, p. 38.
Photo R. J. Milch, New York, p. 47.
Qadmoniot, Vol. 1, Jerusalem 1968, p. 49.
Y. Pinkerfeld Collection, p. 50.
Jerusalem, Jewish Agency Photo Service, p. 51.
Jerusalem, Jewish National Fund, p. 51.
Photo Albert, p. 51.
The Architects' Collaborative, Cambridge, Mass., p. 55.
Photo Bill Maris, p. 55.
London, The Lubavitch Foundation, p. 57.
New York, YIVO, p. 60.
Jerusalem, Keren Hayesod Photo Archives, p. 61.
New York, Oscar Gruss Collection, p. 63.
Photo Frank J. Darmstaedter, New York, p. 63, 70.
New York, The Jewish Museum, p. 68, 70.
Photo Levi, p. 68.
E. L. Sukenik, *Ancient Synagogues in Palestine and Greece,* London, 1934, p. 72.
Courtesy D. Urman, Israel Archaeological Survey, p. 75.
Photo Zev Radovan, Jerusalem, p. 76.
Encyclopaedia of Archaeological Excavations in the Holy Land, Ramat Gan, 1970, p. 77.
Damascus, Museum, p. 81.
Photo R. Cleave, p. 81.
Worms, Staedtische Kulturinstitute, p. 84.

COLOR CREDITS

119